D1715409

Sprouting the Curriculum:

Perversely Logical
Thoughts and Essays
on
Improving
American Education

J. Lockwood White

ISBN: 979-8-35091-550-1 paperback
ISBN: 979-8-35091-551-8 ebook

With steadfast gratitude to brainy, funny, extraordinary Larry

TABLE OF CONTENTS

LOGIC

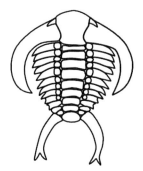

PREFACE

Anyone reading the following thoughts and essays should know that some are before the 2013 buzz about new standards, a situation that Diane Ravitch has punctured in her book *Reign of Error*. (2014). Revealing how much of it is really corporate, the slim or nonexistent gains for urban students, the worship of data, and the not-so-secret strategy to get teachers to compete mercilessly and then calling it collaboration, among other things, she hits the mark with stunning accuracy. Following her lead, I hint at the greed, and then I launch many rockets.

Despite being a therapy chronicle, every thought in this book in your hand, is still cogent, it's all just a little bit creepier now. That said, you will also be subject to many surprisingly boastful, buoyant or comical anecdotes.

No attention has been given to form, the genesis was purely communion.

The following entries were moments when I have had time to sit still on an evening or on vacation to reflect on an experience or condition. They are also the result of dodging asteroids headed my way. They overlap over decades, so that you can see how many different ways a problem or a bonus can manifest itself. Some ideas repeat for emphasis because they arose from different places in different years. They meander clumsily through calm, rough, muddy, and clear water. They are filtered honestly through my humble neurons.

Special notes

1. The word master (from the term "master teacher"), in this book, is meant to denote a high level of creative and pedagogic skill.

2. Some references, subjects, names and places may have further information in the Citations near the end of the book.

Acknowledgements of Teaching and Learning: Glorious Sideways Learning

I thrive as a teacher in a self-contained classroom. I rush full-speed ahead, looking for ideas and implementing them, with the ease of not having to check back with *anyone*. However, I must admit, I also sponge up ideas when in a team setting and I have hit the jackpot with awesome camaraderie over a forty plus years' career in various settings. Polly, Steve, Claire, Diana, Marg, Jackie, Ann, and Chick showed me how to be a natural—how to walk the walk, and make every moment utterly relaxed and meaningful. Every small, seemingly insignificant detail was savored. We plumbed the environment in the "Project" and found many treasures. Their work was like a sheltered, monastic achievement. They created a workplace free of pretension and showy displays. They lived their truth quietly.

Linda, Peggy, Mary D, Mary M, Viola, Betsy, Dot, Ruth, Jane, Patty, and Karen made genuine friendship and fearlessness fly out in every direction. Nothing is harder than running an infant-toddler day care setting. They made it look easy and were able to actually *make* it easy together. They covered Morristown's parks and playgrounds, while toddlers absorbed the geography.

Bonding with their children and each other, those teachers metabolized a unified, obligatory, fun family.

Sylvia, Carmela, Deb, Fran, Linda, Ruth, Mary, Margaret, Valerie, Sister Emma, and Father John had style. The kind of style that kids remember into adulthood, because they listened and responded like real people, not just teacher-type responding. They made the puzzle pieces fit together as every wonderful teacher in that school stopped dead in their tracks at 12:45 and each one of us took a specific reading level to place every kid in the school correctly, reductionist as it was. It was a beautiful thing, very much like clockwork, and it seemed to work. We also partied together at each other's homes and I have to say it didn't even involve alcohol. Although they were probably simpler times, it was the most graceful discipline, which resulted in a rare kind of success.

Marian exuded such warm and sophisticated charm that kids just showed their fullest greatness and cooperation without exception ....and I mean little kids ! Marg made diversity the framework for every curriculum decision and gave meaning to the word "workaholic." Marg and Claire worked without pay for many months. Kathy P. pushed me and supported me with authentic pedagogy and affirmed learning in nature and we weren't even in the 90s yet. She baked bread with the kids every week, (called pretzels) and liberated every idea in her head in the form of captivating storytelling. The kids were absolutely motionless while listening, as she made it up as she went along using their names, of course. Sylvia, the quintessential kindergarten teacher, made quietly simple things extraordinary and gorgeous. Carolyn continues to stop me in my tracks with her unique delivery systems. Sue S, the other Sue S, Lily, Pat R, Ray, Pat K, Judy, Mary, Leslie, Beverly, Alison (The Energizer Bunny), Joan, Melanie, Fran, Ingrid, Michelle, Linda, Ruth, Caroline, Monica, Libby, Dean, Donna, Gabrielle, Rob-ert, Mary Ann, Kati, Katie, Nic, Nancy, Moira, Valerie O, Valerie W, Nina, Mary, Kathleen, Kathryn, Edna, Jennifer, Rosie, Gail, Gale, Heather, Eileen, Sheri, Joe, Susan, Lisa, Sally, Gene, Suzanne, Wendy, Jill, Clau-dia, Ann, Alan, Marj, Joyce, Tom, Janet, Kathy, Anthony and many, many others kept pushing me and sup-porting me in ways you might not ever guess. They tolerated all my ideas and helped me embrace the dream of a nature-based program. They all pushed in new and remarkable pathways that I could wallow in.

Glenn, calmly helped by teaching me the real technology while Billy and Noel translated my old mentality into younger thinking. Sid, the clever orator, kept the darkness interesting, cheerful (hilarious), and moving along. The frantic moments were squashed, corrected, and lightened. Our teaching styles were dynamically different but in some crazy way we were able to support each other. Frequently he would ask me for an idea and I would give him one from MY stylistic bag of tricks and he wouldn't quite say "that's a terrible idea" but instead, it somehow would give him a *different* idea that appealed to him. It was the most interesting process. Sid was the model for loyalty. Mikey and I were partners with very similar teaching styles. I learned with Kathy as a partner that two heads are more energetic than one and Mikey and I moved city mountains. We convinced administrators (especially the awesome JW and YD) to allow lots of field trips, overnights, bobwhite chick-raising (before we knew better), mural painting, garden creation, clubs to connect science to arts, awesome labs, Saturday trips and more. Mikey built thirty fossil sifting screens in one weekend. We were both willing to spend our own money ....lots of it. "You can't wait for heaven, you have to make it," (Heinrich Heine,) was the mantra. I remember the time when the school bus didn't show up for a Saturday trip and Mikey went to the ATM machine, took out cash (his own), and called another company. He taught me to love humanity as much as wildlife. He's a poet, awesome bongo player and lover of spontaneous singing. Everything necessary for good teaching of science.

The following people have shown me the most supportive, positive regard and welcoming friendship as well as insight from committees, field trips, overnight field trips, or faculty meetings: Ms. Greggs, Mr. Niskoch, Mr. Segarra, Mr. Nier, Mr. Szewczyk, Dr. Zelin, Miss Cherry, Mr. Kirchmer, Mr. Adamchak, Ms. Townes, Ms. Gallagher, Ms. Gavin, Ms. Knutson, Ms. Hatcher, Mr. Miller, Ms. DiGiori, Mr. Washington, Ms. Benn, Ms. Martin, Mr. Robertson, Ms. Dentley, Mr. Sabuur, Ms. Alston, Ms. Lipinski, Ms. Howe, Ms. Hudley, Ms. Ince, Ms. Smyth, Ms. Garfield, Mr. Byock, Ms. Yancy, Ms. Rubin, Ms. Hunter, Mr. Jordan, Ms. Thoren, Ms. Neville, Mr. Fashtak,

Ms. Alessio, Ms. Lindor, Ms. Hofler-Mattur, Ms. Adcock, Ms. Newman, Ms. Gaskins, Ms. Haizel, Ms. Shackleford, Ms. Connelly, Mr. Edmund, Mr. Obsuth, Ms. Nelson, Ms. V. Nelson, Mr. D'Angelo, Ms. Hawkins, Mr. Cannon, Ms. Anderson, Mr. Grassie, Mr. Olumbe, Ms. Rich, Ms. Walker, Mr. D'Argenio, Ms. Warren, Mr. Rosenberg, Mr. and Ms. Paterson, Mr. Batchelder, Ms. Serbin, Ms. Dove, Ms. Cordero, Ms. Biggs, Mr. Andrews, Ms. Gandhi, Ms. Gryzwinski, Mr. Djondo, Mr. Sarabo, Mr. Whitaker, Ms. Kelly, Ms. French, Mr. McGeehan, Ms. Bailey, Mr. Pinckney, Ms. Cadet, Mr. Tulino, Ms. Ervin, Ms. Pardo, Mr. Finnegan, Mr. Love, Ms. Murray, Ms. Glandsberg, Ms. Pompilio, Mr. Joseph, Ms. Clemente, Ms. Weiss, Mr. Audige, Mr. Dorcely, Ms. Alceus, Ms. Anderson, Mr. Anderson, Ms. Farley, Ms. Serratelli, Ms. McLean, Mr. Leone, Ms. Truitt, Ms. Facciponte, Ms. Greenberg, Ms. Moore, Ms. Zadlock, Mr. Isaacson, Ms. Finkle, Ms. DeLa Cruz, Ms. Young, Ms. Solomon, Ms. Lopez, Ms. Jones, Mr. Noel, Mr. Felder, Ms.Vasquez, Ms. Antonazzi, Ms.Stith, Mr.Garnet, Ms. Zambrano, Mr.Bernath, and Ms. Lippin.

Rather endearing and helpful security and maintenance personnel always made my teaching experiences decidedly richer. They were the best. They knew everything and gave free advice.

Let's not forget the crossing guards. Ms. Ann and Ms. Dolores, who really spread the love in the community, and that, of course, is a lesson.

Of all "sideways learning", I must include organizations that don't give grades but offer **pure** enlightenment such as the Association of NJ Environmental Educators (ANJEE), NJ Audubon, Great Swamp Watershed Association, Friends of Great Swamp, Great Swamp Outdoor Education Center, Lord Stirling Environmental Center, Essex County Environmental Center, DEP's Sedge Island Teacher Training Center, Genesis Farm, School of Conservation (Stokes State Forest), Wetlands Institute, Stone Harbor, and the full package Geraldine R. Dodge Foundation, who won't give you money and support without transporting you to a higher level first. They trusted me with all their support, services, people, field trips, programs, and training.

In an "after-retirement" temporary gig, strong voices but stronger actions provided me with early childhood performance art. Susan, Jen, Keisha,

Nicole, Kathy, Vineeta, Jarret, Dana, Laura, Megan, Jill, Elyssa, Danielle, Valerie, Nina, Andrew, Maribel, Lori, and Minati have been and will always craft the sumptuous Emergent Curriculum.

Going back to the beginning:

When I arrived as a freshman in college, the graduate resident and the resident director, themselves only about twenty-five to my eighteen years, were the sophisticated but sometimes hilarious models of how to be an adult. Georgianne and Malcolm spent so much time with us and genuinely got to know us. They partied with us and introduced us to their friends, so it never occurred to us to do anything risky. Malcolm was so funny and engaging and Georgianne was so damn smart that we just bonded with them in an unconscious way.

Four years later, Malcolm convinced me to take a year off after graduation, to ski, XC ski, wash toilets, change bed linens, and cook for fifty-five at a ski lodge in Quebec. A lot of learning about business, people, all types of skiing, nature, Quebecois culture/politics, and French language learning happened. Of course, I visited the schools (as I do everywhere else I go). I didn't need to make money as I had food, entertainment (skiing five days a week), and a place to sleep. I'm sure you can imagine that this sounds privileged, and it WAS privileged, but I thought I was scraping by as I knew all I had was my parents' roof to end up under afterwards. Four of us (Malcolm, Kit, Rob, and myself) kept the lodge humming, literally often loud singing, and learning. Even now, half a century later, I think, "What would Malcolm do?"

Of the names I have missed or can't spell, I hope you will forgive me. It's me and my pathological distraction. Trust that our honest interactions were genuine.

Each school setting has its own culture, which shows the highest common denominator as people align and let the weaknesses trail off. Perhaps this is an evolutionary striving of sorts. Each setting providing new things to learn *should* mean greater advantages for children. *Add* to that culture or respect a great one when you see it!

Common Core State Standards' Numbing Effect

As of June 2013, most states have adopted these miraculous benchmarks. We collectively couldn't raise scores with the less vigorous, previous standards, so this can only be interpreted as a friendly, but expensive, warning to teachers and students. "You didn't follow directions, so now your strange but deeper rebuke is to have more punishing directions. After all, Asia and Europe are putting us to shame." It's hard not to be impertinent in response.

Given that there are weak teachers, mediocre teachers, and master teachers, society has fallen to the weary notion that the weakest should be the focus. The Common Core State Standards (CCSS)is a useless response with a numbing effect. The few young teachers waiting in the wings might not last long with so many contradictory and hostile mandates. "Here is your script, follow it carefully." When the script doesn't work, we will punish YOU. Instead of guiding you, we must focus on some serious penalties, which brings the whole ship down with you.

There ARE a few weary/weak teachers. They can be helped. It's not the only problem.

Evolution and Education

Australopithecus was our human predecessor. We also had a few more important modifications before the current *Homo sapiens*. Now we are the only species on the planet with **long**, effortful, childhoods. At first, this does not make sense for evolutionary striving. Large predators can find you and eat you as your baby cries for food. The parent must find the food and contend with the noise machine for a very extended period of time. Whatever the turning point species was, it was an underdog. "Claws" ….not great, strength ….not great, speed ….not great, teeth ….not dangerous, fur ….not super thick. So the brain in one of these evolutionary lines had to get bigger and bigger, shrewder and shrewder to survive. The other hominids couldn't quite pull it off. But for our line, children were invented—born—way too early to survive, with years and years of required support. This resulted in a formidable evolutionary trade-off and the brain, by necessity, achieved full deployment.

Primal, indigenous people (past and present) seem to manage childhood in logical ways. Children grow up, knowing how to be adults that appear satisfied.

We need to do this better in our Western society.

Foundations and Shifts: What SHOULD American Education Be?

Let's start from scratch and that means without politics, as well. What should human offspring be doing all day? If we start with what other mammal offspring do all day and then shift our ideas toward what an animal with a very large, complex, representational, metaphoric brain might do, we might be closer to a meaningful and pleasant school experience.

First of all, baby mammals have the bad luck of being easy prey for any hungry adult fox, snake, red-tailed hawk, etc. It's the top predator's raison d'etre. Do the math. After the two offspring that replace the parents, the rest are needed for the food chain. With that difference out of the way, their missions are to practice living, avoid being targets, learn how to do everything, learn some self-control, develop observation skills, and play around. Ever watch puppies? They do an extra helping of fooling around because they don't have to learn to make a living, like other mammals, but you get the idea. Baby squirrels are weaned at seven weeks and leave the nest at ten weeks. That must be a no-nonsense amount of learning packed into three weeks. Despite their advantage of greater instinctual abilities than humans, they must learn how to dodge or outsmart predators, find safe and nutritive first- and second-priority foods, store food, build shelter, and compete for mates. Now they do have the buffer of sacrificing siblings as they learn their skills but it is still a stunning amount of material to acquire in a very short time. The stakes are hugely high—you slip up and you perish. So this pass-fail school is short and to the point. Back to those dead-beat puppies. Their lives don't depend on learning skills or learning in general, so they get to fool around more. Think about our students who can't figure out why they are endlessly filling in the blanks of material for which they don't see the point or haven't been engaged—they most assuredly revert to puppy behavior.

Now for human offspring. In this country, the model for public education was the Prussian military.

1. Group people by experience
2. Group people by abilities
3. Learn distinct skills in that group
4. All groups change activities after specific periods of time marked by a bell or buzzer-like sound.

It's tidy and it has caught on and has not been challenged greatly, except by John Taylor Gatto, but then mostly ignored.

Traditionally, school has leaned toward the acquisition and manipulation of symbols because written symbols were an elevated way to communicate when this stolen country formed and continued through the point when public education took hold in the 1850s with great thanks to Horace Mann. In European settled America, the language has been English and the code is represented in straight lines and curved lines. Hold that thought.

Harold Gardner, 2006, has developed categories of ways people are brain-wired for different sensorial preferences for extracting information from the environment. He feels that the way people's brains are wired might make them more inclined to prefer (and succeed with) nature activities over reading activities, for example, and that each student would do better if there were a better way to eat from the smorgasbord of: Nature-smart; Musical-smart; Interpersonal-smart; Body-smart; Word-smart; Self-smart; Picture-smart; Logical/Math-smart. There are, of course, studies to refute his theory. At the college level, we've been teaching Howard Gardner's "system" for a generation and still schools won't admit that Word-smart is still the predominant vehicle of transmission.

That said, American Education could mirror the look of savvy pioneer children, logically learning about their surroundings for survival and pleasure. Physics, chemistry, fractions, geography, etc. all packaged in relevance. Keep in mind that within the following, there are many crossovers and overlays, and interdependent superstructures. Here is an outline for logical ways for children to spend the day.

Logical maintenance activities

Chores such as:

Gardening

Food prep

Cleaning

Sewing

Recycling

Maintaining equipment

Fishing, hunting, shopping, selling

Tending to shelter maintenance

Helping with the "family" business (homeschoolers)

Maintaining a weather station

Maintaining a school store

Raising "butterflies"

Projects

Develop a homemade weather station

Garden development

Fundraising (educational and meaningful), not junk peddling

Physical skill development

Archery, gardening, preserving food, cooking, sailing, skiing, fishing, sewing, bike riding, individual or team sports, hiking, hunting, Double Dutch, etc.

Intellectual skill development

Water quality, air quality, species counts, vernal pool monitoring, citizen science

Mental exercise (pushing symbols)

Language arts, math, world languages, history, civics

Field Trips (fishing, hiking to habitats, stream studies, visits to local historic sites, museums)

Sports

Individual: kayaking, bicycling, gymnastics, fishing, Double Dutch, cross-country, kite flying, sailing, etc. (competitive or noncompetitive)

Team: soccer, hockey, swimming, crewing, softball, lacrosse, basketball, Double Dutch, etc. (competitive or noncompetitive)

Arts (paints, sketching, fibers, jewelry, glass, clay, etc.)

Music (Listening, playing, singing, bird-calls, etc.)

Literature: Humans love story (depending on age: storytelling, picture book stories, chapter book stories, short stories, essays, poetry, lyrics, etc.) With *no* strings attached, please.

Crafts (real crafts that are age appropriate: spinning, weaving, woodworking, basket making, felting, crocheting, etc.)

Research (primary or secondary) trade books on information, internet, etc.

Action Research (attending surveys of individual local interest and gathering data)

Social studies (current events, civics/large or small community, geography, history, especially local history)

Science (to underscore the above with highlighted concepts, formulas, etc.)

Pleasure (learn the physics of skateboarding or bicycle mechanics to enjoy your ride)

Your environment (the names and qualities of *your* trees (yard or street), plants, fungi, animals, rivers, climate, bedrock, soil, etc.) because they're YOURS and you rely on them

Your economics (the interrelationships of what works for you as a child but also as a neighbor, family member, school member, etc.)

Teacher's favorite hobbies (If the teacher is a birdwatcher, it will be contagious with students; if the teacher's passion is collecting pictures of bridges and naming the construction style of bridges, rest assured, it will also become the passion of her students; if the teacher loves mystery novels, chances are that will spread to students.)

The overlooked truth is that the school day has gotten so far from what's good for kids that it's embarrassing to be human. Squirrels and whales are fully aware of how their young offspring should spend their day despite the fact that infant mortality is high for them. Even in the best schools, authentic development comes hard. Advanced life from other planets would scratch their heads (if they have heads) trying to figure out what the hell we're doing with our kids.

We're mostly just pushing straight lines and curved lines. This is ok for those who are inclined, but not acceptable for those who don't have enough experience yet, or desire to use them representationally, and they will just mix them up and give up. This is not a small percentage of children.

From the Trilobite

From the humble trilobite, came many new adaptations as well as a sense of staying true. Those fossil-hunting field trips are so much more than they seem.

Meteors

I am a teacher. I don't "shop" or do my nails or decorate my house. I teach from every angle, through current events, bird migrations, weather reports, or the history of slavery. I used to wear a meteorite necklace which broke the chain because of the weight of the iron. Luckily it happened one morning before I left the house. Read between the meteors.

Wait

Wait ....I'm from outer space ....those creatures are making their offspring symbolize information...that they haven't learned yet...?

The Brink

At the beginning of this century, because of revelations in brain research, there was a hope that schools would actually turn around and teach authentically. That is, do what young humans need to do for five hours a day, five days a week. I use the word revelation, but master teachers have known for a long time what kids need to do, and they have done it. However, parents are nervous about the authentic approach and the giant education industries power up the dogma ....selling stale, snoozefest learning, such as "rubric education" and differentiated instruction. Also "data-drivenness" has got us by the throats. Scrutinizing international student achievement, the U.S is not impressive. Great teachers know where their students need to go. We are now spending tens of hundreds of hours assessing and evaluating instead of thinking of great activities for *our own* students. Curriculum is handed down from arrogant strangers. Yes, there is a need for memorizing. Yes, there is a need for worksheets. Yes, there is a need for lectures. All approaches are necessary but the greatest need is *doing* something that engages.

Why does the dogma persist? Why do the "for-profit" education industries **prevail**? Why has lousy teaching practice metastasized? There are many answers here but one that addresses all types of settings from urban to country schoolhouse is the illusion of control. Control is a powerful word. At the same time it is an extremely delicate thing. Students vs. Teachers. School Boards vs. Administration. State vs. Feds. Then throw the cards in the air and reshuffle. The hope is that this word can be forgotten and a stronghold of great teaching practice can come to the forefront.

I have a veritable relationship with simple truth and I am going to tell it. Please listen.

The Learning Hemorrhage

Cutting to the education chase of why anyone cares about schools in the first place, is the curious proclivity to worry about reading, but more specifically, decoding. This country has spent an obscene amount of money on reading programs and reading research. The solution is so crystal clear that there is no other conclusion about the problem than "no one wants a solution" because many people would lose jobs and philosophical substance.

Organically, children's eyes are not the right shape for reading until roughly age seven. A corollary is that writing requires a seven-year-old hand as well. My own non-empirical, forty-three plus year career take on this phenomenon is not so much the organic readiness but the need for that age group to **care** about others' thoughts in code. The cart is before the horse.

The proof that this urgent course of study is a pathetic waste of time, literally, is that program after program gets rolled out decade after decade, and significant numbers of kids are unsuccessful with each iteration. If there *were* productive outcomes, there would be no discussion.

Instead of focusing on the actual learning of the world around, from age five to seven, we continue to require children to represent the facts they haven't learned yet.

What is the definition of insanity?

Weep or Enlarge

Of all my teaching experiences, I will take this opportunity to weep for the mediocrity, or expand on the transcendent practices of a few of the settings in which I've had the privilege of working, some with more emphasis. The current setting will always be more acute, exactly because it's current. The greatest focus of this work is on an urban middle school, an urban fifth grade of a K–5 school, and a free form Nursery–sixth grade private school in a middle class neighborhood which I founded and ran for fifteen years. In total, I have been a teacher for forty plus years and no two years have ever been alike. I keep tinkering. Tinkering with imperfect models is foolish and yet when it is the only option in the exhaustion of frustration, "micro-crafting" takes on urgency.

We make our human offspring endure artificial training five days a week for their entire childhood because it's "good for them." No other species farms out its young with such serious determination.

On some issues mentioned here, I slam with my opinion and on others I leave it up in the air for the reader to ponder. No two classrooms in the world are alike—more detailed than fingerprints. The dynamics and possibilities are exponential as are the comfort zones for learning.

Yes, this is in part, a shameless storm of various strengths and weaknesses; just a random, disconnected, verbal film of my interactions in the world of education.

CONSTELLATIONS

A Hexagon Is Formed in Nature

"Why don't you give us parties?"

"Hmm ….what do you mean?"

"Our last teacher gave us candy every Friday, and soda and cake and cookies once a month if we were good."

Now that New Jersey's governor, John Corzine, signed the law removing candy from all public schools including birthday celebrations, we will separate the men from the boys. Who can teach without treating kids like jumping seals and who simply can't. Consider the fifth grade teacher who is trying to teach in an enriched academic culture. Since kindergarten, the children have been given candy rewards sometimes at the end of the each day. In middle school, it's given at the end of the period, so the next period teacher, gets them "all sugared up" despite scientific claims that this is not true. Teachers would welcome researchers to see for themselves. How does that set up the new teacher who wants the kids to appreciate subtle understandings like poetic imagery, the beauty of how a hexagon is formed in nature, or complicated lyrics in a song? For her, those *are* the rewards. It's an uphill battle to wean kids off candy once they're conditioned. Or consider the class who has a music class first period. They are given candy for good behavior, then returned to spend the day with classroom teacher. She has to deal with effects of sugar and the nasty attitudes over not getting rewards. Additionally, how do these behaviors relate to the swollen rates of diabetes and morbid obesity?

A Rebuff Is a Rebuff

What about the days when a teacher is not at the top of his game? I tinker enough that hopefully there are not many of them, if any. But still, things happen, and imperfect scenarios may just even be someone else's perspective. Our schooldays memories have incidents that felt lousy but were not intentional. We can't dwell on it but we can't forget it either. A ratio of one adult to fifteen to twenty-five students will render a "miss" now and then. Hopefully, teachers are forgiven. In many cases we don't even know it happened. We hear, "That's life; they'll get over it!" But toughening up little lives should be minimal. Teachers need to be aware because everyone has a different take on any action. Any rebuff is really a big rebuff. There is no assurance of impunity. Stress is the trigger and there may not be any mercy, and the result may be a tiny scar.

Acceptance and Status Symbols

In the education community, we try to teach students to be accepting of all cultures, habits, customs, routines, and pathways. It's hard not to release an exploded giggle when something is very different from what we are accustomed to.

So when I look at photos of my childhood from the 1950s, I try not to recoil in horror or scream with laughter at my mother and aunts all wearing complete foxes tied around their necks while dressed for church on Easter morning. I try not to think of how barbaric it appears to be. I try not to remember that I was accustomed to it as a child; and try not to think about how pathetic a practice it is for middle class people to want to show that they are more than middle class.

Without integrity (think: integrated) in life and education, we are reminded of how easily you can slide into a comedy (of errors).

Accepting Guidance and Criticism

I have been doing "conscious" teaching for over four decades. On my teaching art, I seek criticism, confirmation, and affirmation from various people. Here's who I look to: people who are also teachers... NOT people who have **_left_** the classroom. Not supervisors, administrators, specialists, and hold the phone, not program trainers from profiteer companies. Why did you leave the classroom? That's the big screaming message. You LEFT. Why should we follow the guidance of someone who chose to leave it? If you were so good, why didn't you stay? It makes no sense at all to listen to you. Be honest. You're not in the classroom because you wanted to get out. Accordingly, I cannot respect you in *any* way. Mr. or Ms. Workshop trainer, you are dishwater to me. Just dishwater.

(During and) After the Pandemic …. Any Pandemic

I have yet to meet a parent who is now a **_strong_** fan of any online or virtual learning. However, hold that thought because it does have its benefits and I will honor them below. The main point is that virtual can be a snoozefest and young bodies need to construct knowledge for:

1. inspiration, 2. retention, and 3. self-motivation. They need to move and BE. They need to be in the world putting all the parts together literally and figuratively. That's the truth for authentic learning. Having a live teacher and being in a matrix of students can be fun when it's not bullyish. Alternately, for symbolic encoding, which we all eventually must do in this post-modern world, having awesome tutorials that a kid can REPLAY over and over

as necessary is extremely helpful. The kid is thoroughly in control of her learning. One of my tutoring kids has been fine without me because of this. If a child is the victim of bullying, virtual learning is a *relief. (*But this is not the solution to bullying. We all need to eliminate the causes which promote bullying. When kids have real things to accomplish all day, there is very little bullying.) Sadly, "lame" is the label I apply to the outcry that "the children have lost learning time!" . The data crunchers in June 2023 have now alarmed the greater U.S. that the kids are many "points" behind. This was declared on the Solstice of all days. If we valued every moment in life and appreciated all our activities, children can and will construct knowledge from vacant lots to weather study. Everyone has birds flying overhead; everyone has shadows; everyone has health situations; everyone has clouds and physics. Alas it can not be measured ! Everything can be studied in depth. If a family did not plumb the greater constellation, shame on us.

Altered States of Mudpies

Serving up some mush from wet mulch, a dollop of creamy, wet soil and a sprinkle of gritty sand, a kindergartner will stir vigorously or dreamily and then gradually space out. Spacing out can be reinterpreted as "focusing in." Sometimes humming or singing lightly, this unmistakable altered state is formidable. It's challenging to get the child's attention. Something is going on in there that is very powerful and ripe. The intellectual bliss is palpable. Interference would be ….anathema. Fostering the altered states of mudpies allows a mental infrastructure of greater and greater rewards. A rich, private, deliciously complex inner foundation creates bursts of shapely neurons that just can't help connecting with each other. In 1977, Dorothy M. Hill wrote *Mud, Sand and Water,* the teacher's bible of how to see kids lose themselves in the highest level of creativity and sublime satisfaction with the purest of Earth's basic materials. Oneness with transformative materials is the money in the bank for intellectual and emotional mileage. Just watch a fifth grader rearranging rocks in a stream to create a new channel.

Play, true play, is the "highest kernel of human consciousness," according to Edith Cobb, in her masterpiece, *The Ecology of Imagination.* Adults disrespect this in a respectful way. It's just the clunkiness and expediency of the grown-up brain. Take them to the beach more often. Be willing to do more "tick checks," so they can dig holes and use sticks.

Always, ALWAYS, see the other side ....be the other side

This was a tough year (2016) with Mr. Trump blindsiding everyone, but mostly pollsters. Democrat or Republican? In my naïve corner of the universe, I believe that dichotomies might be dangerous. We are never going to have world peace if we can't break this down and always see the other side. How greedy to only look at one's own needs. See the "other" side. Really look. As a teacher, I need to immerse myself in the challenges of the administrators, see what's best for the school, **and then** see what's best for me. Right on up the food chain to the state overseers, examine their challenges, then work together to do what's best, pinpoint the greedy, lazy weak link, and work to fix things.

Here are a few very diverse examples:

As the employer of Sprout House, a small private school, I knew how prohibitive it was to give employees long stretches of leave, paid or unpaid. Bad for kids, no padding in the budget. I had to see the needs of families, but also wanting to serve underpaid twelve-month teachers is a struggle.

Workplaces closing and moving out of the country cannot be swept under the rug just because it's not your workplace.

As a public school union member, *I* know it's unreasonable to be able to retire at age 55. That's stealing from your neighbors. It would have been much better to fight for higher wages.

Trump supporters have legitimate grief. Pick it apart and help them. Run a mile in their skin, shoes, and diet. We must.

If we don't practice seeing the other side, world peace is like a white tablecloth. Looks good at first, but it won't last.

(Forgive the preaching.)

"Animal Farm"

The school building has three floors, each with two wings in an L shape. It's a large building; one wing is old with a marble staircase, brass banister entrance, and the other wing was built just a few decades ago. Approximately a hundred adults spend the day here between teachers, administrators, para-professionals, office workers, guidance counselors, cafeteria staff, custodians, security officers, and one police officer. Additionally, there are always visitors. At the corner of the L shape on each floor is an adult bathroom. The faculty room has two bathrooms. There is another bathroom near the auditorium. There is one in the main office and the nurse's office. These are singleton bathrooms, not rows of stalls, thankfully. Do the math. There is sometimes a queue at the start of the school day, and before and after lunch. It's a miserable feeling to be on that line, knowing your students are waiting for you in the hallway. It was a stunning move when an assistant principal closed the second-floor bathroom, for her own private use. Protests were ignored.

At the End of the Day

Corporate evaluations are based on what a person produces in large part. How they produce it is also important, but decidedly secondary. There are many tangible ways to assess the results. Products are products and services can be well-documented. Not so in American Education. At the end of the term*, teachers **do** get their students' scores on state tests, but never get to see the testing instrument to see if the evaluation is fair or match students to questions, in order to improve teaching style. Corporate settings have straight-forward, no-nonsense regimens in general, compared to education settings. I have no idea how the standards play out on the test but it shouldn't matter as long as I cover the standards. The problem is not seeing the presentation of standards and relating it back to a particular student. In a business setting, you are profoundly aware of how you fell short on your product or service. We **do** get the category and type of question, but that tease is profoundly disrespectful of what rookies and master teachers alike are trying to do.

* In my district, to receive test scores, we can only go online during the summer or wait until the following school year. By that time, the teacher is focused on new challenges.

Attrition

Instead of getting rid of bad teachers, current policies actually get rid of best-practice teachers.

If I'm right in thinking that the majority of all kids do best in an environment that is authentic and "content-rich," the worst teachers can still flourish. They are good at manipulating and presenting data in a flash. They know when to reward kids surreptitiously with a warning that an evaluator is coming and a plentiful-candy, homework-free evening will follow. That at least takes care of the "announced" evaluations. The "middling level" practitioners can dazzle with a power point that hits the marks for everything except actual retention. They can make fun of the kids in the faculty room, but buddy them earnestly in person. They look at the bullets of the evaluation requirements, and then hit the marks flawlessly. The teacher folks who want to present a full picture in a deeper context get bogged down in what they're doing and forget to look at the bullets because they are thinking about neuro-diverse learners. The slicker teacher has a prepackaged "diverse learner" plan always at the ready.

Worst of all, the good teachers are adopting the bad teachers' practices to stay alive.

Bad Teachers—Three Types

How can you tell where one problem stops and another starts? This ultra-fine line is most blurry in troubled schools, but the following three scenarios can and do occur in any school system."

1. A weak, possibly new teacher is in a room with strong, clever comedians for eighty minutes (many major subjects are now double periods). That could be the end of the story but I'll go on. The teacher tries to introduce a lesson. One or two people who

are not in the class enter the room. Everyone laughs. They are asked to leave and of course they continue to do what they please. The lesson doesn't get off the ground, and I mean the ground. A climate has been established in that class that's almost impossible to change. A mediocre teacher morphs into a bad teacher just to stay alive. The teacher might resort to incentives (sweets, homework coupons, worse) just to get through a textbook, and hands-on activities can become an abuse of materials with a weaker teacher, *if there is even **an attempt*** at hands-on activities.

2. Some humans are lazy and of course some of those humans become teachers. Bare classroom, chumminess to win over students, and "vocabulary fill-in sheets" are substitutes for genuine pedagogy. Kids will get sucked into this relationship and lose the dignity of demanding their education. This is a popularity contest, not a profession. My mom used to call this type of relationship "a kiss and a promise."

3. A "foldable" is not hands-on education. Some personalities are just not ever going to be adept at finding the courses or workshops that set them up for greatness. They can't find that inspirational *half step for leading kids* from where they understand a concept to a hair above it, to the next level so they don't get lost and frustrated and give up. They have trouble getting kids across the finish line. It's a baffling and heartbreaking matter of motivation on the part of the teacher.

The three examples above can be isolated or combined. (I have no idea of the effectiveness of my colleagues' craft, but judging by how much help, humor, and eye contact they extend to me, I'm guessing they are more or less great.) The "bad" teachers usually last a month.

Further degradation occurs when the new teacher tries to actually give life to the required paperwork. by creating an authentic curriculum, only to be humiliated/forced into following "the script".

(The following are qualifications that are currently standard for many American teachers.) PLEASE READ EVERY WORD, ESPECIALLY THE END, for maximum inspiration.

Job description (of the narrator)

1. Lesson plans written with three-part objectives, activities, higher order questions, labs, anticipatory sets, differentiation, assessments, individualizing for English Language Learners /Inclusion Special Ed students, closure and more. Due every Friday at 2 p.m. (These are not helpful to me, they are just for show—taking two to three hours per week.)

    1a. Revise lesson plans immediately every time intervention is needed.

    1b. Maintain a minute by minute agenda pre-posted on the chalkboard.

2. Grading of papers for hundred plus students daily.

    Include one corrective comment and one complimentary comment.

3. Progress Reports or Report Cards with comments for hundred plus students every six weeks.

4. Carry and bundle textbook material **for 120 students** from the main office, carry to my third floor classroom. This includes a twenty-five-page booklet, quizzes, tests, and study sheets (for 120 students). This is the equivalent of two large boxes but they are not separated. They are all mixed in with other grades and other same level teachers, so these materials need **to be counted and found from six or more boxes.** This takes more than one prep period and if you are not the first teacher to get to the boxes, things get mixed up and the time frame increases as does the frustration level. This activity happens for every new unit.

5. Nightly calls. Issues arise daily. At least two families are called every night out of 110 students. These phone calls take fifteen minutes or more. They include the record-keeping required with each phone call.

6. Provide written classwork/homework for suspended students at a moment's notice.

7. Provide written classwork/homework for Intellectually Gifted students when they are pulled from class every other week for one period. Notice is given. The Student Growth Objectives (SGO) scores of those students who miss these classes are still calculated in my SGO score even though they miss class.

8. Meet with science and grade-level colleagues.

9. Extra, random "Occasional Assignments" from all types of administrators and facilitators such as:

    – Take the twenty "Blood-borne Pathogens" video course and sign for it.

    – Take the "Chemical Safety" video course and pass the test.

    – Create a lab manual for the science department from given materials.

    – Download the Faculty manual and read in entirety. Be responsible for knowing it.

    – Read RESPECT curriculum materials and implement now (no notice) during science class.

    – Complete an assignment and share with thirty colleagues at a district science meeting. This is NOT a turnkey assignment, which is also required where applicable.

    – Analyze and implement directives for Special Ed students and IR&S paperwork.

    – Read Employee Handbook "in its entirety."

    – Submit handwritten rosters within twenty-four hours for two homerooms for Nurse's Office clerical needs.

10. Keep abreast of all records of the mainstreamed, inclusion, and resource room Special Ed students.

11. SGO Preparation mostly during the months of September, October, and February but should be revised and kept"up-to-date" during other months: Excel spreadsheet of all 120 students with analysis in 6 categories. Math calculations analyzing the large group and a specific group with accompanying paperwork.

12. Create poster-like Anchor Charts for classroom display and a Word Wall. These should be current.

13. Three bulletin boards per year—

    • Boards must be on display by the due date listed in the Bulletin Board Schedule. (Changed to several days earlier in the prior month)

    • Boards must display work representing a predominance of one class (80 percent or twenty work samples).

    • Boards must contain work from each class taught.

    • A standards-based rubric must be displayed on the board. Review for grammatical error.

    • When applicable, drafts and revisions that went into the creation of the final product should be displayed under the final product.

    • Each work sample must contain feedback, either directly on the product or on a post-it note. The feedback has to contain one constructive comment and one complimentary comment. Please place the rubric performance level on the back of the final product.

    • Work must be grade appropriate, standards-based, and rigorous.

    • The board should be visibly appealing (i.e. neat, organized).

    • Subject area, class name, and teacher's name must be on display.

It is imperative that the work posted represents the rigor and high expectations we are maintaining within our classrooms. It is expected that you meet all requirements listed in the Faculty Manual.

14. In addition to the hallway bulletin boards in #13, display student work in classroom with rubrics for students' work. Dates on work should not be more than twenty-nine days old.

15. File work for hundred plus students constantly, daily/weekly.

16. After a formal evaluation, teachers are required to write six answers to open-ended questions within forty-eight hours.

17. Create benchmark exams.

18. Teach myself Excel after two demos.

19. Buy my own Excel program.

20. Apply weighting system on all classes in the Powerschool program for every marking period.

21. Item Analysis: After benchmark exams, 360 (120 students X three open ended) questions must be analyzed and data distributed across a spreadsheet. Multiple choice must be done as well but is less time consuming if scantron (automated grading) is utilized.

22. New students (which average about twice monthly) take an enormous amount of time to process and acclimate. This disruption adds to the negative classroom climate and the workload. In addition, these students need to take SGO tests. The EXCEL spreadsheets must also be adjusted. Their scores on teacher's evaluation depend on the number of days of attendance.

23. A new mandate requires that the booklets (text that goes with the Smart Board Technologies program, of which I currently have no Smart Board !) when complete, need to be "archived" in plastic binders for each student and stored in the classroom. I have over 100 students. The plastic binders which were defective to begin with last year did not last very well. Out of 120, twenty-four were functional but not in good condition. I gave about ten to the special

ed teacher and about three to students who asked for them recently in November, after seeing them taking up space all of Sept and Oct on a shelf. I have about ten left so the archiving is not possible even if there were something to put in them.

24. **MY Full-time job! PREPARATION OF wonderful, interesting, engaging activities and lessons for hundred plus students. This includes shopping/paying, scrounging, lugging, setting up, cleaning up, filing, photocopying and dreaming up how to pull it off. There is no overlap with the written lesson plans in number one. Those are stilted and artificial and geared to some other subject, probably Language Arts. Large amounts of planning are involved since the science PSI program is all lower order questions and lower order concepts.**

Since it's not humanly possible to do this job description, do we assume we're all bad teachers?

Barbaric practices

Since troubled school settings are often places where a fire starts before the previous fire is extinguished, a person doesn't like to criticize, and yet someone's got to snap out of it.

Enormous amounts of money are spent on preachy programs such as drug-scare assemblies, incarceration-scare assemblies, marches, chanting, red ribbons, and sugar-laced parties. Boring afterschool programs and boring camps are the norm. The answer to almost every bad-behavior issue is lockdowns. Punishment mentality is crippling and the desired outcomes are barely even temporary.

Wholesome positives get shot down. All this money could be spent on kayaking adventures or a sailing camp or cooking school. I've done adventure experiences for forty years with no accidents, so please don't tell me it's dangerous.

When life combusts in a failing school, you can't help feeling that it's at least a healthy sign of students reacting to specific injustices. The problem is how simple the solutions could be.

Belle Terre (I Gave Up)

I gave up on Sprout House when I realized two things for sure after fifteen years of trying. It was never going to be diverse, for whatever reasons, and I was never going to be able to pay teachers a living wage. I was literally discriminating against single teachers with a one-income household, and ignoring children in concrete and cement environments. For a while we had a relationship with the R.E.A.D.Y. (I believe it stands for Rigorous, Educational Advancement for Deserving Youth) Foundation of N.J. where our teachers volunteered to take kids from the concrete environment, on stream studies a few times a year on Saturdays. That ended after two years when the foundation thought the activity wasn't academic enough.

Heartbreakingly, I closed our Elementary School, but passed on the kindergarten, Nursery, Childcare, and Summer Camp to the very capable and dedicated teachers and board of directors. Some of our Elementary students didn't find good placements, so I promised I would create a "One Room School House" for one year for those students, which we named Belle Terre. We averaged six students through the year and it was a wonderfully pure and transcendental time of learning. We spent a lot of time in the tops of very tall pine trees at the edge of the parking lot of the church where we rented a room. There were a few acres of wooded area at the back of the parking lot. This setting was perfect. Our classroom was half below ground and opened out into a patio behind a stucco retaining wall. We could just spill out the classroom door and do our work in a protected area outdoors. It was a singular space for doing projects—the ultimate protected patio. Projects were geared to our weekly field trips in which the wonderful parents took turns driving. We scoured every habitat within thirty miles and many farther. From animal migrations to the Revolutionary War sites, we lived it. But my hope to work in a diverse setting was still there.

Benediction

I Pledge allegiance to the Earth
To the flora and fauna
And human life it supports
One planet
Indivisible
With safe air, water, soil,
economic justice, and peace
For all

I've seen many iterations of this benediction, with many people taking credit. It doesn't seem to be William Sloane Coffin as I had originally thought. Regardless, here is the point:

Lawyers are true to their clients. Medical doctors have an oath. Environmentalists *are* an oath. It's a mandate that teachers have some kind of benediction, any kind, but mostly self-approval and immersion-blessedness.

Blank Classrooms

When you see a classroom with one poster demonstrating something about a subject, rules about classroom protocol, large-size rubrics, computers/interactive whiteboards and not much else, one must assume the class is:

    a) discussion-driven

    b) fill in the blanks–driven

    c) technology-driven

    d) combinations of the above

I know I would lose my mind as a young student in this setting. As an older student, my arthritis would kick up.

I believe a great teacher could probably make an empty, blank classroom work, but they are few, and I would suck at it.

A classroom should look like a workshop, museum, an oasis, a theatre, a comfort zone, a library, an art gallery, etc. Just as people have vision for their homes, a teacher can capture a year in the life of a group of kids and make it an awesome memory without preachy, gaggy posters from the teacher store that scream "I just slapped this on the wall; I'm not really a career professional."

My room starts out with boatloads of activities, cocoons and wildflowers (planted and cut), and gradually evolves with some messy projects in all stages. How could it not with 110 students? When outsiders first enter my room, they *squeak*, "Wow." I'm not always sure whether it's always a good "wow" but I think it is.

"You can't wait for heaven, you have to make it"—Heinrich Heine.

Blue Ribbon School Districts

The stress of attending a blue ribbon school district is rarely considered by young couples selecting the location of their first home. They make the proverbial beeline for those communities. They read the stats for Ivy League college placements and SAT scores. Mind you, they are probably not even pregnant yet.

Fast-forward eighteen years. Some of those offspring, who did well in school, even if with tutors, have a nasty habit of dropping out of college before May of freshman year. That data is never easily available when young parents are searching out neighborhoods before their children are even born. School districts don't advertise it. Why should they? It's not on their watch, so it's imperative, in competitive districts, to guard against this particular form of stress and anxiety. Of course, there's also the factor of helicopter parenting contributing to this phenomenon.

Brainwashing

Kids' brains align with their teachers' brains. Neurons are "plastic" we are told and I look at my students in March and realize that they are little versions of me in our private little science culture. They ask questions that interest me and start to prefer activities that I prefer. I see it every spring and start a controlled but numb, grieving process, that they are soon (next September) not going to be my little nerd-clones anymore.

From the small, subtle details to the complicated architecture of twenty people living in one room together, certain routines or non-routines are mandatory and will imprint on each psyche in its own way. The environment, rich with personalities and concepts to be ripened has compelling depth and scope.

Being in a hands-on classroom molds the brain to be profoundly proactive. Being in a note-taking classroom molds the brain with more emphasis on organized reception. Both are valuable but the neurons become differently shaped. Having students for only one year is a tease and at worst a waste of time for lifelong skills. Rich classrooms are a powerful milieu formed by the teacher and framed by the students. You take the ball but if there's not enough time to run with it, it could be an exercise in frustration or apathy.

A seventh grade teacher says to me, "Even though you're a good teacher, your students have no more skills than the group who had a sub all year." Gee thanks. Maybe it's because they're stunned that the next class could be so boring and lifeless and they give up.

Brooklyn-American

I can't believe there is no word for the ethnicity derived from Irish and Italian parentage. Brooklyn, NY, was full of us. Most specifically, the baby boomer cluster. Additionally, there should be further nomenclature for which parent is which. It makes a difference. Now that Irish-Italian combo might have had a little more drama when it first started fusing, but I missed that part. It was a *very* normal phenomenon by the time I was a conscious human being.

Brooklyn gave me friends of every stripe. Words and food from many backgrounds could be found in every house. It was a given that there would be English tea in one apartment and latkes in another. I admit it was a very white neighborhood, but in the next apartment building, the super's family was Black. He had a daughter my age. I was dazzled by how competent Gwen was. One time when I played at her house, her mom invited me for lunch. I guess we were about seven or eight. Gwen just stood on a chair and started scrambling eggs. I was flabbergasted at her skills and that her mom gave her autonomy.

I happened to be taught by large numbers of Socialist leaning Jewish teachers who absolutely smothered us (in a good way) in what was called "Brotherhood," and gigantic hopes for a strong United Nations. We hung out at the UN building. Honestly, it was a mandatory field trip and I can't remember how often. Maybe my school happened to attract this group but maybe the movement was larger. (Come to think of it, Bernie went to the same elementary school !) The teachers with Irish sounding names definitely fostered the Brotherhood curriculum with gusto as well. Neighborhood and school: the cohesion felt very normal. I guess the kids took it for granted. We honestly didn't see dads as much as moms; but the moms looked nothing but comfortable with each other.

One of my best friend's mom, who was a conservative Jewish lady, would wake me up for mass if I slept over. We were tight. It was also probably the first generation with so much cousin diversity. I wouldn't say "no two cousins were exactly alike," but there was definitely diversity at family parties.

As I look back, I gasp at how barely historic the holocaust was to my childhood. It felt like grim, ancient history but it was recent! Everyone must have been in pain, but as children, the adults shielded us. Looking back, there was a semi-stoic treatment of the subject, allowing and fostering very happy childhoods. And so I can only conclude that I am a very lucky and secure Brooklyn-American. Isn't everyone?

Bruce Wilshire

Bruce Wilshire, in his book, *Wild Hunger: The Primal Roots of Modern Addiction*, 1998, has encouraged a compelling look at the post-modern condition.

When children are in a natural setting like a meadow, they will approach with hesitation for anywhere from two to eight seconds. Then they might run, dance, or do a cartwheel. Examination comes next. "Hey! Here's a spider!"

Except for those who are fearful (intrinsically, or much more likely *taught* to be fearful), the rest are getting pumped up and naturally high. Yes, literally high. In the book, Bruce Wilshire talks about the flooding of endorphins when humans are present in the generosity of a Natural setting. (It's an evolutionary throwback to equating the scene with resulting food and/or the rush surrounding the hunting process.) Wilshire talks about "finding regenerative ecstasies"; in other words, self-motivation so that endorphins don't ever get cut off.

Endorphins get short-circuited when something artificial provides the rush. Our students get short-circuited when teachers give them candy rewards or worse. Schools where the culture is sometimes "Six Flags" instead of "Museum of Natural History" have to unhinge an ingrained mental framework. The lingo in many schools contains phrases and words such as "incentives, classroom money, detention buy-backs, pizza party, and homework coupons." Alas, we've missed the boat when we help design neural networks in kids' brains that look too much like a rat maze instead of a map toward a self-actuating fireworks pattern.

In the Sprout House elementary setting, all age groups of kids were immersed, literally, in woodlands, streams, rocks, soil and seeds in an unassuming equilibrium. It was the backdrop for all other symbolic learning. It was the backdrop for life. As far as I know, there have been no incidences of substance abuse.

Why do most people give a quiet but positive sigh when they come upon a waterfront scene, a view of a lush forest, or a wide angle glimpse of a mountain range? Humans are programmed to feel positive when they see a cross-section of Earth sans commerce or construction. It signals a place where food can be hunted or harvested. The possibility of which brings enormous relief, richness, and/or pleasure.

Schoolkids who have just taken a field trip to a rustic stream setting, profit from that experience with a rush of endorphins. Later that day, or on a subsequent day, they learn symbols with a more relaxed satisfaction or simply learn content by extracting information out of that very same environment. In addition, meaningful visits to natural settings provide **layers** of information because habitats are *systems* that make sense and can be applied to facts, or facts can be applied to the system. In other words: authentic learning. It's really no big revelation that abundant experiences in natural settings are a giant boost to the education of any child or adult for pure academic facility *and* less chance of artificial chemical dependencies. Surfers, mountain climbers, wild edible foragers, and cross-country skiers might try recreational drugs, but probably won't have any dependence on them. Lacking empirical evidence, I am convinced it's the Zen truth.

Cake batter and grout mix

What principle in physics keeps those little powdery balls very dry, preventing the cook from attaining a creamy, smooth, homogeneous mixture? One millimeter in diameter and tough as nails, outsmarting the mixer. Unless attention is given to each individual clump, they remain defiantly intact. When teachers do everything right, find the developmental level, use engaging activities, know their students, focus on the positive, monitor the quantities of materials and make it process, not product, to name only a few strategies......some students are still completely lost. Given all these attempts, brain research tells us time is the missing element when all else is still a struggle. Time is a gorgeous luxury. The cake ball and the stubborn grout ball will finally be absorbed in moisture. Even the troubled kid who has seen and experienced trauma will let information seep in as it becomes more and more relevant. Unfortunately, time is not one of the menu options during the reign of programs like Race to the Top, No Child Left Behind, etc. Gimmick du Jour is the only reality.

C.A.P. Corrective Action Plan

My principal evaluated me on April 13, 2014. She is required to give me feedback in a conference in no later than three weeks' time. Three weeks elapsed, then four. Nothing happened even after I inquired. I was told that "she would call me." But instead, on May 1, she vanished. No letter came to explain her whereabouts to the students, parents or staff. We were introduced to an interim principal on or about May 5 (a retired principal from our district).

Our principal appeared again June 2 all cheery and confident. She caught up with me two days later. "You have a choice: keep the eval from April 13, or I will do another." My response was, "Do I get to read it?" With hesitation, she responded, "Ok." I went to the office to read it. Again I was told, "She will call you." Another ten days went by. At that point I got an email to arrive at her office for a pre-eval conference. I enquired about the previous eval and the options I had been given. "It wasn't good; let's do it again." It was now June 13 and the last day of school was June 20. We discussed my proposed lesson to be evaluated, which incidentally was after the final exam, and I went on my way getting ready for a 9:07 eval the following morning. She didn't show up for that. During my cafeteria duty, in which NOTHING can be heard, a colleague came running in saying, "They're paging you." Upon my arrival in the main office, office staff are breathlessly telling me, "You didn't do anything wrong." My response was "I know that; what's going on?" The office folks continued.,"Ms. C. came to evaluate you; we had your schedule wrong. Be prepared for her to come eighth and ninth period. Since all the grades were in, my lesson plan was to design schoolyard habitat brochures, which would take the kids outside and keep everyone happy; hopefully every-one. Ms. C arrived punctually and was dazzled by the lesson, the engagement, the questions, the obvious previous mastery, and the effort. The evaluation, however, was not the top grade of "4: Distinguished," although the actual lesson part of it rated a four, it averaged only a "3: Achieving." If I had the time, I would have contested it. That piece of it is extremely loaded.

Long story short, the science supervisor now had to do a "summative evaluation" on me during the first period on the very last day of school, because he was required to wait for the principal's eval. The night before, I checked my email before I went to bed (necessary evil) to find an email from him saying I needed a Corrective Action Plan (C.A.P.) because I didn't achieve the necessary ratings. I was stunned and reeling, sick to my stomach, and unable to sleep. I am such a cocky, confident teacher I didn't bother to learn how to calculate the ratings. My husband sleepily said, "Not worth the worry. Go to sleep; it's got to be a mistake."

Mr. Supervisor showed up at 9:00 instead of the agreed upon time (8:25). "Did you get my email?"

"Yes," I said, "and it was very disturbing. Please do the math for me." He asked for a calculator. By the third calculation, he said, "Oops, I was working with a spreadsheet yesterday, not doing the individual calculations." My students were lined up at the door for the period starting 9:07. So much for a summative eval or an apology, or respect for students, but goodbye C.A.P. Some of my colleagues weren't as lucky.

Cash Cow/Regime

The Failing Schools Regime is a new industry that doesn't listen to the master teachers in that particular failing school or the administrators with insight. It is a way for retired administrators to claim a lucrative post-retirement job on top of their pensions. Therefore no one with the real power really wants the failing school to go away. Are they responsible for the failing school? Of course not, but it fell in their laps as a fabulous windfall. $250–$1000 per diem isn't pocket change on top of a pension. Stunned and secretly happy, they gladly accept these wonderful part-time assignments to inspect classrooms and write the reports. Does the governor realize this phenomenon? Probably not, but his large staff that oversees the part-timers are fully aware of their raison d'etre. This piñata is shamefully excessive.

Less career-driven teachers will opt out of the system to be "trainers" to complement the former administrators. Why not? The nightly three hours of grading and lesson plans are **gone.** Any tricky behavior issues are **gone.** This reduction in stress will add years to your life.

This failing school industry will be hurt if schools turn around. Read Board of Ed minutes and see what they charge for one day of trainings. Nothing they do is bad, and in fact, the trainings usually are good practice. The problem is that they become a script that master teachers are insulted by and weaker teachers just can't implement. Both groups can't stomach the paperwork, flow charts, graphs, pyramids, pretentious jargon, and pretentious lesson plans. This is to justify the costs.

Failing schools are a lucrative industry.

Failing schools are a windfall for the education industrial complex (that isn't milking the charter school market). Specialists get $1000 dollars a day on average. Administrators just have to show "the state" that they are implementing something new when the scores don't rise significantly each year. Teachers' heads spin as programs are dropped for the next ones. Just keep rolling them out. Teachers must do the paperwork (homework) for the trainer before the next workshop **on top** of all their other normal paperwork (see job description). It's almost all gimmicks but even if it weren't, the students are hurt by the abrupt changes. No one cares and the system continues because it's lucrative. The trainers win and the administrators continue to get their very decent salaries despite the bewildered students in the classroom. My guess is that that frustration manifests itself in unrelated, unconscious bad behavior days or weeks later.

(Studies Take a Look at) Charter Schools

Blah, Blah, Blah! There is endless hashing and rehashing of charter schools.

Ok. Can we stop pitting public schools against charters and vice versa? The laws prevent charter schools from selecting higher-level students and/or refusing low-performing students, which is always the allegation.

Here's what really happens. The lottery or open registration system for the charter must follow the letter of the law. So far so good. The students start school. The well-meaning charter school has established high expectations or they would not have been granted the charter. Many of the low-performing students cannot meet the expectations of the charter and receive failing grades or are fatigued by the workload, longer day and/or longer year, detentions, long detentions and Saturday "breakfast clubs." The magic pill the parents thought they were taking does not pan out.

They drop out. No one expels them. They show up back at the public school. I know this firsthand. Last year I got eighteen students back from charters (out of 110), some only spending a month or two in the charter. Now they are really lost because of differing curricula and can't succeed very well at all. In addition, I lose many top-performing students mid-year because they suddenly get an opening in a charter school.

This is a very subtle statistical challenge. Instead of blaming public school teachers for their "low showing" in impossible conditions, we should think of ways to keep the best models afloat; and I don't mean scores from one year. Long-term college acceptance/RETENTION would be a better marker. Case studies would help in the short term.

That said, I am soberly worried about corporate charters, their methods, their profits, and their teachers struggling with the quandaries of being vastly overworked. The most revealing data shows the short careers of those teachers. It's nearly impossible to profit on quality education. It is decidedly problematic to make a profit on insipid busywork. It's also very hard to make a profit on schools in general. Be suspicious.

Civilizations   (Sometimes it's therapeutic to just write a poem)

A troublesome flaw
as civilizations are
concerned.
Answers are in
streams limping through
forests and the "setting" star
not setting when you climb
the hill
or the spark from flint
under and around the baking bread.
Celestial bodies do not have
liverworts in training and ...
That cold front over there
brings essential wind for the
elegant technology of the kite

while the warm front rises instructively,
where civilizations are concerned.

Colleague Accepts Different Answers

In subject areas where there is no state test, teachers are required to collectively develop their own tests at grade level to test students. The tests are given first in October and again in March. These subjects are of course science* and social studies. The opportunities for irregularities are exponential. These are subjects where a choice has to be made to test the October unit or the March unit. Of course the March unit is selected because the objective is to show an increase in scores. The students won't have any idea of what the answers are in October but will have great familiarity regarding the same questions asked in March. This schema is perfect fodder for bewildering and demoralizing kids in October and demoralized kids don't do well in general, therefore hurting potential scores on state tests.

The students aren't the only ones bewildered and demoralized. Of the 122 students I started with in September, 101 were still on the roster by test time in October and seventy-seven were still on the roster by test time in March. Three had withdrawn and returned weeks/months later. There are weighted calculations for days students might be suspended as well. I can't tell you the formulas for calculating my success/failure rate as a teacher because I needed so many helpers to walk me through it.

We developed a very good test with essential questions. These questions connected with many units. The multiple-choice questions were good framework questions. There were no stupid tricks. I didn't mind reviewing because the basics were there and it could be applied in various ways. A colleague, however, had one bad evaluation (see "evaluation day") and decided to give the students the answers. This is a natural progression in a system such as this. Stay with me here. I was surprised as heck that her students did much better than mine, because sixth graders usually get things twisted when they don't really understand them. But the joke was on me because although mine did better on the open-ended question, hers did better on the multiple choice.

The following is what I did to explain myself:

Narrative for Specific SGO (Teachers must explain themselves)

"In the interest of higher-order thinking, my expectations and preparation for the specific question were rigorous. The students approached the question as a yearlong guideline for many areas of science. I considered the question multi-faceted with the need to apply many different principles showing understandings of almost all the different units we covered. In addition, I prepared the students with activities for this question in all of the "multiple intelligences.""

My focus group contained sixteen students down from twenty-one. I graded the question with high expectations and fairness. Six students met the complete and comprehensive expectation. Eight students met the partial expectation. Two students met minimal expectations."

The following is the answer *I* expected from my sixth grade students:

Why Does the Earth Appear to Have Fewer Impact Craters Than the Moon?

Earth and Moon are very close in the astronomical neighborhood, so according to the reasoning of scientists, they are equal targets of space rocks. The Moon appears to be covered in craters and Earth does not.

Earth has an atmosphere that burns many space rocks (asteroids, comets, and meteoroids) before they land. The moon has no atmosphere to burn space rocks.

Earth has oceans on a majority of the planet, so many space rocks that do get through the atmosphere, disappear in the ocean.

Other space rocks that also get through the atmosphere and hit land might be visible now or could have been in the past. Over time, tectonic plates move a great deal, changing the surface of the land. Lava may have covered craters. Slowly moving glaciers may have had a grinding effect. Weather and erosion also smooth out evidence of impact craters. Living things grow right through craters and make them hard to see. Finally, human construction of roads and buildings could have destroyed craters.

I found out later that my colleagues simply accepted "atmosphere" in a well-developed paragraph, as the answer.

* Only eighth graders get a state science test.

Common Core Evaluations

My new common core evaluation is this week (2016). I am told that I will need to answer six long-answer type questions immediately after and return the document within twenty-four hours. In a previous training, we were told that as a result of the evaluation, we would be labeled 1, 2, 3, 4—4 being the highest. This "4" is called "distinguished" and it was only something to strive for but never achieve.

One of the questions we must respond to is "how could I make the lesson better?" On my last evaluation, I responded that I put my best effort into that lesson and tinkered with it until I got it right and therefore had no improvements. I got it just the way I wanted it. Surprise, I was told that that answer wouldn't be accepted. The logical outcome: strive lower.

The language in that evaluation was detailed, flattering, and had no negative recommendations. My rating: "3 achieving."

COMMUNICATION

There is so much bullying about writing. When I taught fifth grade, my language arts supervisor informed us that our students were required to write ten sentences in their journal every morning. I had two students out of fourteen who could write a sentence. I had eight students who dutifully put periods anywhere around any words in order to count the number of sentences. Every sentence had multiple spelling, grammar, punctuation, and capitalization errors on a large scale and I could sort of get the gist of what they were saying but it often didn't make a clear point. I had four students who wrote almost a full page of letters and punctuation marks. One of these students could read it back to me clearly and make a beautiful point. This obviously was an official learning disability but I was told that by October of fifth grade, it was ridiculously late to process through special services. Regarding the two who could write fine sentences, one did a great job and was a jolly fellow. The other would often put his head on the desk and say, "I don't want to do this."

"Why?, I asked."

"I don't want to say anything."

Sometimes when I supplied topics from which he could choose, he would comply. More often, he did not. A professor of mine, Dr. Michael Knight, used the term "crap detecting." My reluctant student had excellent crap detectors. Writing is a profound experience about communicating something to people known and unknown. Encoding something for big audiences is not genuinely on the radar of ten-year-olds. I have enormous respect for the kid who wouldn't write. Communication has the same root as communion. It's a warm and fuzzy sharing. My student wasn't feelin' it.

Comprehension Reading

Although ticking off each phonetic letter-to-sound symbol in American English (or any language) is very reductionist, kids who learn through projects and real life, will not mind it. They will see it as a puzzle or matrix and it will most often come off as fun.

My seven-and-a-half-year-old homeschooled grandson has simple little booklet stories created by an unusually straight-forward, non-glitzy educational publishing company. With only black-lined sketches, each story/booklet is devoted to one phonetic concept. As you might guess, we are not talking about Barbara Kingsolver–level literature, but each story has something of a twist ending and something to chuckle about in the middle. On some level, my grandson knows this is not the quality of books his family would normally offer, but he looks forward to the activity, maybe for a somewhat effortless sense of mastery. I get to smile when I listen to him reading along and he will add an appropriate adjective to make it better or delete a clunky article.

When I tell him he should read it exactly as it is, he makes a face and asks, "Why?" My answer is that this type of book is for learning phonics, and he has been known to do the head shake as he makes another perplexed face and says, "Alright ….alright." This is what's known as comprehension reading. He doesn't read each word haltingly; he searches for meaning.

His mother, at a younger age, told a friendly adult that she had "read" a certain book. The friendly adult said, "That's very high-level reading!" I had to explain to the adult that when my daughter referred to reading, she meant, "I absorbed the story …." even if someone else read it to her. Decoding was just a detail. No need to rush it.

We are lucky to have a system/list of phonetic skills in our language. **When the time is right,** kids will breeze through them. It shouldn't be a new form of child abuse.

Corona (W)holistically

Our reductionist world is similar to our reductionist schools. And a reductionist school can be related to a plant that's been bought at a garden center. I love garden centers but we all know the success rate of the things we buy there is not 100 percent. When a plant is taken from its own microbiome, full of its own bacteria, viruses, fungi, invertebrates, etc., it's taken from its own private pharmacy; it can't shop there anymore when its needs and conditions change. Many, if not most post-modern, schools are not rooted in anything but a smattering of various subjects and skills that might be needed in adulthood. There is no microbial mat or matrix or integrated root system in many cases, except "future success." That is not necessarily a bad thing, but if there is very little respect for a current, underlying system, it might be a problem. Kids who just have "parts" are not living/breathing a "system" and may look at their environment as separate objects that don't go together. Learning is about how something *big* works. When one "part" changes, everything else must adjust. Noticing how a change affects everything else is the wonderfully unconscious learning.

The only object that should just be randomly "plucked" is a trinket in a souvenir shop. Even art in an art gallery is speaking to your experience, so you buy it and pull it into *your* system.

Humans have been treating the planet like a bowl of trinkets. I want this and I want that: oil, gold, slaves, titanium, lumber, silicon, not respecting that they are part of something else. When the planet gets ripped apart, we get climate change. Warming temperatures foster serious diseases. Factory farms foster pollution and problems with ocean health. Habitat loss brings animals in contact with the wrong systems. Everything is out of whack. Insects can take easy advantage. So the invisible killers aren't really invisible at all. It's not a matter of science saving the day if the planet can't function without an artificial vaccinating jumpstart. "Quickie science-fixes" just push off the problems to our grandchildren. We need to root ourselves in the complicated firmament. We can't keep grabbing for the easy fix and rendering ourselves into tinier and tinier pieces. The easy fixes almost always come back to bite. Holistic can be spelled like "holy"—spiritual or spelled as in "whole," indicating a healthy system that works. Complicated diseases are a symptom of environmental degradation.

Corrective Action Plan (CAP) and Gifted and Talented

From September through December, my highest performers were removed from my science classes on a rotating "pull-out" gifted and talented program. This included all but one class, two or three from each class. It happened about every third week but our classes are double periods. **Any** pull-out program is upsetting to science teachers. How does a student teach themselves "endothermic reactions" or "series vs. parallel circuits?" Rarely did anyone come after school to see the material as I asked **and** that would only be for a shorter version. The lab materials are usually somewhat cleaned and organized by then and no one wants to stay very long.

In a school where attendance is a monumental challenge, how does a pull-out program (gifted and talented, speech, special ed, etc.) make any sense at all?

Now I have to say that these children are great thinkers and problem solvers, well-behaved for the most part and really enjoyable to be with, but they realize somewhere during sixth grade that they must also be cool, and staying after for a lab isn't that. They will also be the second (not first) to stampede to a fight to be a cool spectator.

Along comes the March SGO test and these wonderful students have gaps in their knowledge base, which doesn't kill their scores, but the bruises show. The teacher is, of course, rated on the outcomes. My colleagues are suffering with CAPs and this is part of the reason. Although I don't have a CAP, my scores showed it as well.

Crushing Harm to Children

It is December 2013, in urban New Jersey. The mental and emotional suffering of the children and teachers in this ridiculous climate of an urban middle school is numbing. Although it started around 2006, when it became apparent that "children were still being left behind," the crescendo is now manifest with two teachers hospitalized and death of two teachers—all stress-related in my school alone.

For their elementary years, students were confused by "rigor." They were subject to the great mishmash of "challenging" academics. Work they couldn't do, like "find the area of area of a circle", before they could find the area of a square, or solving a two-step word problem before grasping multiplication and division was the emphatic trend. Writing a ten-sentence journal entry every morning before leaving first grade is another stunner. One of my colleagues was put on probation because markers were found in her room. (Markers are not rigorous.)

In middle school, the top 25 percent must be gifted to survive this confusion of "so-called" rigor. Of this group, most will pass the state tests in sixth, seventh, and eighth grade. The lower 75 percent will wander hallways with a restroom pass, disrupt their peers, turn their God-given intellect into humor and showmanship to continually hide the conscious or unconscious hurt of having their time wasted; that scar is going to follow them for a while. Add to that the almost daily testing of some kind, lack of time for teaching the material, one hour warnings for excessive paperwork deadlines, expectations for constant email checks, 120 students per teacher, and bizarre, twisted, sometimes dangerous student behavior. The paperwork and phone calls associated with unacceptable behavior is palpable. With a required classwork and homework assignment per day, the teacher has 240 papers per day on top of the 120 practice tests that are almost every day. The formal lesson plans, the real lesson plans, and the endless stream of the data-worshipping item analysis for every question on every test. The progress reports, the report cards, and the rude rebukes from administrators are not just flawed and impossible; it's a pathological assault on teachers who happen to be human beings. There are now no evenings and weekends and endless, perennial teacher assessments of "not effective." Teaching is now the occupation from hell not just because of the treadmill workload but for the crushing harm to children.

Culture of Interruptions

In my current middle school classroom, there is a daily bombardment of interruptions.

A few years ago, there were "pull out" vocal and instrumental classes. "Your students will only miss one class every fourth week." Over my d*** b***. This is a major subject (not that a minor subject should be missed either), so with so much worship of test scores, wouldn't it make sense to have the best shot at them? Now there are "pull-outs" for Intellectually Gifted (IG) classes. This makes no sense. We're studying exothermic reactions, which will be tested and IG is building bridges out of popsicle sticks. *I* am punished if my students do poorly on *the test.*

Then, there is, of course, the eye doctor, the ear doctor, the scoliosis doctor, the guidance counselor needs messengers, the language arts teacher is inviting a student to her pizza party, collections for various causes, unannounced assemblies, the police need an eye witness account of something, a student from a previous class forgot a book, a parent appears in the doorway, the fire alarm is pulled for no reason...(the worst year? 21 times in one year) and checking on the substitute teacher next door when the noise becomes deafening. How about the grant that was written for a Shakespearean company to do a performance, only to be interrupted by a routine fire drill? Why were they scheduled that way? Why wasn't the fire drill changed? It happens when a school has no office calendar. The same thing happened for a live hawk and owl program that cost $600. Luckily there was a tip-off at the last minute so the birds could be packed up safely and quickly before the fire drill. Imagine how this works on kids in failing schools. The frustration and disappointment becomes manifest in a variety of ways (that's another book). These interruptions are nothing compared to the electroshock type jolt you get when the office staff is barking an announcement over the intercom. My students conducted a three-month tally of announcements where there were "whole building" messages. There were on average 3.1 interruptions per forty-minute period.

Compound this with the rate of "tardiness" (5 percent daily) and average attendance (79 percent daily overall) over a two-year period. These are my figures from my classes.

Tardiness and absenteeism are another form of interruption; perhaps the most pernicious. There are so many variables here but so much room for improvement.

Curriculum Covid

It's September 2020. It would be the perfect opportunity for the freshest starts. Many people are staying home and keeping their children home. However, instead of embracing real-life learning, the children are mostly being subject to canned, packaged imitations of the dead curriculum that their textbook/powerpoint publisher inflicted. Always plodding, with or without a face covering. There's a lot more learning to be had if we just watched the street pavers all day from start to finish. (Hydraulics, chemical changes, physical changes, wheels, physics, money, taxes, safety, etc.) The education industry has a tight monopoly on brainwashing and product lines, even though we *know* the current model only works for a certain percentage of kids.

I can't even imagine what it's like to be in the school building with a mask on. Teachers say the tiny children's masks have circles of moisture, not to mention that many children are encased in plexiglass. This is a very tough solution to needing socialization when we are worried as heck about mental health too. The establishment is too stressed to notice the missed opportunity.

Damien is Working on His Math

Damien is working on his math, having sneaked the high and low temperatures out of the Star Ledger to calculate the average temperature ahead of everyone else. The first one finished gets to put it on the chalkboard. He takes his temperature graph out of his folder. The slightly rumpled graph paper has a line graph any fifth grader would be proud of. His hand is raised to put his calculations on the board, I decide to call on someone else; someone who hasn't done it ahead.

Damien is staring at me quietly. He's got the right striped polo shirt and the right jeans hitched at the required low level. He's meticulous and neat. His millimeter-long hair is newly clipped. His notebooks, folders, and books are neat inside and on top of the desk, all the time, unusual for a person who has only been around the sun eleven times.

I announce that we will move to the next activity and I shuffle a few materials of my own. Everyone knows the routine and begins to move. I look up from the things I am moving, and Damien is retracting his foot in mid-air, halfway to or from Thalia's foot, which is under her desk behind him. She is still engrossed in her journal on her desk, so I surmise that his foot was still on the way or he hit the leg of the desk instead. He looks at me with eyelids stretched guilty and questioning, but frozen on me. I return a strong, steady look, hoping it conveys no communication except that of pure surveillance. He slowly puts his foot down. I am unsure of the reason for the slow motion.

"Use good judgment, Damien," I say quietly.

Looking frequently over his shoulder at me, he moves to his science activities around the room: evaporation data, worm food preferences, beetle life cycles, telescope time, checking for spectrums under the window prism, watering citrus seedlings, listening to the slug terrarium with the headphone amplifiers, recording barometric pressure, comparing the homemade barometer reading to the digital weather station, microscope work, shell sorting, checking the bird feeders, etc. After, or during, each stop, he has something to tell me that is not significant; he just keeps reporting back.

"Miss White, Miss White, the Woolley bear is at the top of the terrarium."

"Miss White, Miss White . . . nothin' ate the suet."

This is not his usual style. He usually blasts through, eager to see what's going on, with little or no concern for me. Today, since the "leg lift," he is all over me.

It becomes circle time, our town-enforced "Anti-Gang-Drug-Violence Initiative." We clean up to get ready.

"Can I get the chairs?" he asks. I look at him long, but not as long as I stared when I saw "the leg."

"That would be good," I say slowly. After some squabbling over the chairs for a minute, we start with today's questions. I happen to disapprove of this crap, so I'm hoping for an acting award.

"What's your favorite movie? Why is it your favorite? Is there any part of it you don't like?"

The kids are all smirking, as if to say, "This . . . is an excellent time waster." I feel like *my* fifth grade teacher, thinking, "Wipe that grin off your face!" Next agonizing question: "What's your favorite food?" We go around in the circle and not one person hesitates with their answer: "Cheeseburgers, collard greens, fried chicken, macaroni and cheese." We get to Damien, who also does not hesitate:

"The snack you made for us."

"Which one?" I ask.

"The one when we read poetry to Mr. Gembel and Ms. Novalis" he says quietly.

"Oh," I say, "does anyone remember it? It was way back on Halloween."

A few voices pipe up, "Apples, yogurt, and that stuff."

I clarify, "Apples, yogurt, and granola."

"Yeah that's it," he smiles in his brilliant, fawning obsequiousness so I will forget all about the attempted kick. We continue with the other kids. No one else mentions this snack. After a few more questions, it's time to conclude with the Anti-Drug-Violence-Gang PLEDGE . Damien stands, but he will not condemn his own parents. He looks down in silence.

And I silently pledge to use good judgment.

Data-Driven Programs

Data mining is a thrilling pastime for artists, social scientists, psychologists, mathematicians, gardeners, and stockbrokers. Being scrupulous and detective-oriented affords fascinating angles without even being tedious. It's like searching for fossils—you dig forever and then you find an amazing scapula with a slightly different shape or density. The methodical nature is comforting because it makes it hard to make a mistake.

The luxurious amount of time playing with these details is not cheap. Education in any country simply can't afford to trade one or two salaries per district, telling teachers to focus on predicate-adjectives when the money could be spent training that teacher to grow sunflowers in the school garden or learning how to construct a windmill. Look at the data. Ha ha, I mean look at the schools that really work. Kids are engaged in awesome and understated projects that really motivate.

At the end of the day, the good teachers knew the weaknesses anyway and are taking care of them, when they don't have to do triplicate lesson plans. Leave the mining to the geologists and paleontologists.

"Debating the Use of Drugs to Curb the Abuse of Drugs"

Wha—?

Front page *NYTimes*, December 30, 2018. Now that's a plan. Use drugs to curb drug use. If outer universe intelligence gets a whiff of this, we deserve to be embarrassed and ignored. The rationale is convincing because the death rates speed by like cars on the Long Island Expressway. Please, please stop the madness. Rehab needs to look more like health…kayaking, hiking, art, music, fishing, exploring.…….Forget thinly disguised preaching and talking and listening and talking and feeling and talking. We've got to get out of the box; we've got to get out of the insular, circuitous system.

Easy for me to say, because I've never felt the torture of withdrawal, and so going humbly full circle, I realize how important it is to feel good *in order* to work through positive approaches.

However, if the positive approaches to healthful activities and schools that make sense prevailed, we could ditch this idea so that the only thing OUTSIDE, outer-space intelligence gets to be amused by is the indoor skiing at the Xanadu Mall in NJ.

Depleting the Teacher Force

All the data crunchers are not making a loud enough blast regarding teacher attrition. Young teachers are exploding out of their buildings, some not even making it through the first year. You name the reasons or look at my essay listing bullets of my job description. This phenomenon strikes me as a crisis on steroids. No teachers? What do we do then? Imagine the chaos even *on the way to* absolute zero. The fuzzy gray years when class size soars but isn't quite criminal. All the twisted little behaviors (students *and* teachers) for coping will snowball, as trouble remains more or less subtle to the administration that can and will wear blinders. They have no choice; the answers must come from a different level…..the public.

Discipline and Playfulness

The behavior in my sixth, seventh, and eighth grade school reminds me to worry about the toddler and early childhood years of my middle-school students. Who was confined in a punitive preschool? Who had to endure a boring nursery school? Who sat in front of a TV all day most Saturdays? And who sweltered playing on a cement or black-topped play yard all summer? Some parents lovingly craft every moment of the day, which is another stark problem.

You don't have to be a psychologist to know that whatever came first is influential, formative, or possibly downright scarring.

What is behavior like in certain middle schools? I've experienced quite a few schools. It's bubbly and enthusiastic. Students are eager to construct knowledge. The curriculum, whatever the current morph, is almost always dead and stale, frustrating, slaying, and twisting the most stunningly beautiful, positive energy. When age-inappropriate, silly playfulness is a strong driving force, make no mistake about the message.

Also in an understated way, remember that discipline's root is disciple.

Dominance and Brain Athletics

I broke my dominant right hand when I was teaching "third graders," in an alternative setting. I actually broke it hiking on a field trip a mile from the parking lot. I had no pain, just a little fear, so when the kids heard frogs on our way out of the woods and begged to investigate, I let them stop with the chaperone while I continued on to meet the emergency transport vehicle.

At the time, cursive writing was at the beginning of its fast-death spiral, but I was determined to keep it alive in my corner of the world, so when I got back to school four days later, I taught cursive writing with my left hand in large strokes on the chalk board as usual. It was really no different from how I would normally do it with my right hand. It seemed silly, but nothing more. That was nothing compared to all the tasks in life that required my left hand to do things it wasn't used to. Button clothing, mix ingredients, brush teeth, turn book pages, drive a car, open windows, open drawers, "write," rake, etc. I kept thinking about the people who were also in my boat that knew they would never regain their dominant hand and so I appreciated that my situation wasn't so bad. Sometime around the fourth week of this existence, I had strange mini-episodes of feeling surprised by myself: my reactions, thoughts, and solutions to problems seemed strangely parallel to my usual ways of interpretation and expression. They weren't hyper or sluggish, just different. I felt remarkably unrecognizable to myself, but shrugged it off. The strange cloud persisted and I sat back and enjoyed it, because the actual physical ordeal (recovery from surgery and metal pin removal) was a bit grim. The fact remained that I felt like a weird stranger to myself/body. I was definitely somebody different. By the seventh and last week before the cast would be removed, I found myself to be again able to grab the refrigerator handle with my previously dominant hand, unconsciously. The right hand was almost recovered. By the following week, I was sure my old reactions were back as I used the right hand progressively more and more. It was very dynamic, not just a little change. The ghost of the left-handed me was gone. The old me was back in a very odd way. It wasn't trauma that caused the dichotomy; it was my hand talking to my brain.

Draw your own conclusions. The take-away for me is the enormous hold physicality has on learning and the endless possibilities there are in the realm of school settings and programs.

Entrepreneurs vs. Socialized Education

Public Education in America is like Socialism or really more like Communism. In 2013, when we have so many tragically failing urban schools, shouldn't it be time to get rid of the Socialist/Communist model? Public education should employ "owner-operators" (but not literally). Each teacher would keep students for two to four years for every subject if the individual were a renaissance-type person or alternatively, just for their subject. They would be forced to truly invest in the kids, work up to the state test, and the ring of "capitalism" would echo fairly. Fairly, only if the teacher were the sole decision-maker for every material, program, lesson plan, and mandate. No teacher bullying. No profits, no corporations, but a very comfortable salary. Objective, outside entities provide an entrance test on day one; then the exit test again after "two" years. You swim or you sink when it's over. The current model of "you're fired if they don't have adequate yearly progress, but we won't let you do what you think should be done" is hilariously absurd. There will be no teachers left with the current, obscene dogma.

Essential Wisdom

Newsletter April 2005

Dear Parents,

Every day is Earth Day at Sprout House, but we like to take the marking of the date to help ourselves remember details and educate ourselves. In our lifetime, the last primal people will have come and gone. When I was a child, there were about eight primal cultures that were still just beginning to be infiltrated by nosy researchers. Some of these people still don't understand that there is an outside world, although there are surely parts of their communities that do interact with outsiders. Even so, they are reluctant to change much, if any, parts of their rich and satisfying lifestyles. This is not just a whimsical, saccharine musing; we need to pay attention to the fact that they are so sophisticated that one of these groups outsmarted the tsunami in December. Our so-called advanced civilization could not. It is indeed a crucial turning point in the history of the earth to be about to lose this essential wisdom. We'll never get it back.

Evaluations of Teachers

In my school, we're teaching eighty-four-minute periods (on alternating days) this year. This is great for hands-on science. There's time to gather materials, complete an activity, clean up, and record whatever is necessary. In my school, we account for *every minute* on an agenda posted on the wall or chalkboard that is written before the class starts:

Example

May 15

"Do Now" 7 minutes

Current Events 6 minutes

Readings 14 minutes

Collaboration 4 minutes

Partner Lab Work 22 minutes

Lab Report 9 minutes

Learning Centers 19 minutes

Closure and Explain homework 4 minutes

Since mastery and autonomy are huge parts of successful learning, my job is to read my students' minds and allocate time with their best interests, or survey them the day before. This leaves the teachable moment in powerful disregard.

When the evaluator enters (usually someone who wasn't even born when I started teaching; see "Why are you an Administrator?"), I could be in the middle of "readings" or "lab report". He or she might stay for twenty or forty minutes. The evaluation report might criticize for lack of relevancy (missed the current events) or formative assessments (failed to see that a lab report is an assessment and that the information was **applied** to the activities in the learning centers).

When we are asked to design an eighty-four-minute experience, it's got to be pretty damn great to hold middle schoolers' interest. Why is it fair to evaluate only a slice of it? Some very low results have surfaced for my colleagues, prompting them to counsel any young teacher-prospect away from the field.

Every Kid Should Have

Every kid should have meaningful ways to spend the day in the "school" season, and a place to swim in the summer. Whether it's a clean stream, ocean, lake, or pool, it's an easy baptism. Effortless floating or a transcendental dunk puts us back in the liquid molecule of our planet's most engaging achievement. The wonderful properties of the liquid provide freedom and proper sensuality! The pretense of leaving the ground is thrilling and serious at the same time. Buoyancy is a momentary alternative consciousness, and I imagine is an extremely healthy time for dendrites and terminal fibers to have a luxurious stretch. I know that "beach-going" is a relatively new human activity. There is no question that some people dislike the practice altogether. They don't like gritty sand, excessive sun, cold water, hot water, etc. I maintain that all children would do well having the *option* of trying this experience which tests solids, liquids, and gases against the skin as a sublime type of stimulating fun. Careful observation of people at the beach reveals a setting that probably demonstrates a very different side of that person's normal activities. Imagining them at home or at work is likely to be an odd contrast. This very alternative temporary habitat draws out risk, experimentation, pleasure, satisfaction, and playfulness.

A day at the beach is not about a strong purpose. A day at the beach is for the release of therapeutic dabbling and drifting. The school week should have some random intellectual stretching and dabbling too.

Every Year Is Different and "The Unfolding"

The hope is that all teachers think new and exciting activities every year, carry their students in their "pockets," and are moved by new trends and environmental experiences. More than that, a propensity to sniff whatever is in the air and bend the curriculum in and around it, creating materials along the way, is the hope of all people who think about children and humanity.

In addition, everyone with high hopes for children wants teachers to get feedback from their students for activities that are right for them and specifically interesting to those *particular* students.

If those conditions are met, a classroom experience would be a carved-out existence; a genuine fingerprint where no two could possibly be alike. Dynamic combinations of people and activities are a lesson in itself. Create an environment that makes you happy. "Don't wait for heaven, make it yourself" is a concept I read about from a translation by German philosopher, Heinrich Heine. In addition to how beneficial that is to kids, the awakening itself is the appeal for teachers. Every year is a new reality despite the sadness when they leave. You live a distinct existence for one school year and then it's over. It would be interesting to see some kind of brain diagnostic of a master teacher of twenty-five years compared to someone with equivalent years in a steady office job.

I tell my graduate students that what seems like a mystical ability or just a remarkable coincidence is the practice of *falling into* the materials you need. This singular experience happens consistently, rendering it a phenomenon rather than a coincidence. I like to call it "the unfolding" or "divine strategies." When one item after another presents itself for the classroom's current subject, you gasp a little and then you get used to it. It's either cosmic or all those things were always there before . . . and you just missed them (as one of my fifth graders suggested). That goes for pre-Internet. Post-Internet is even easier. For example, thirty years ago, when I first started a Lenape Native American activity, I happened to notice that there was a recreated Lenape village in Waterloo Village. The next night, my neighbor happened to show me his arrowhead collection. The following weekend, I watched an arrowhead chiseling demonstration by chance, as I was walking through what I thought was a flea market. Later that week someone I knew was reading *Dickon Among the Lenapes* by M.R. Harrington in front of me. At a garage sale a few days later, I picked up a set of animal skins.

Another time, on a smaller scale, I went to a workshop on multiplication readiness. I realized that the throwaways at my house were all I needed to make all the materials and create new ones. It was a subliminal focus on arrays; the same item laid out twelve times maybe in 3x4 rows or 6x2. I found appropriate magazine ads and clean and interesting discarded items that could be made into posters or displays, sometimes with the help of a copy machine.

If you think this is only about junk collecting, it's not especially, although junk collecting is a very high art. It's about meditating on your students and dreaming up environments for them. If there were a teaching gene, this would be it because it doesn't feel like effort; it feels more spiritually automatic, crazy as that sounds. I know there's a god and I know she loves teachers.

So every year *is* different, in part, because of *the unfolding.*

Factors of Poverty???

Anecdotes

1. A student has a wonderful interest in birds, snails, slugs, graphing growth, tallying each individual find, hypothesizing its success in a terrarium, writing about them, etc. This is pure academics. It's hard to nitpick his grammar in his journal, when his vocabulary is superlative; his ideas are powerfully scientific *and* poetic at the same time. The grammar corrections have to be done or the teacher will be hung. The student is also low man on the social pecking order and will do negative things for approval from his peers. He spends about one day in ten totally miserable, acting out, withdrawing, refusing participation. The other nine days are productive with the right teacher (encouragement).

2. A student sits quietly listening in class 100 percent of the time. His body language tells me he is getting it. He often answers questions and often asks great questions. He does lab work well. He works well with any partner or group and never complains about others. This student never does homework or studies for tests/quizzes. He always seeks me out when absent, for the homework assignment and frequently comes after school to get an assignment that he forgot or lost, but never does it. When asked, he says he did it but left it home.

3. Good kid, happy disposition, two-parent household, plus low income still equals moderate chaos. "Look at me, look at me, listen to me, listen to me." Inability to bear the teacher giving attention to

someone else, resulting in nonstop interrupting. These syndromes can make a teacher's head spin. Blissful chaos is still chaos.

Feast for Thought

For some reason, I do not worry about random space rocks hitting Earth, even after the spectacular wake-up call in Russia in 2013 or the numerous small misses that always seem to whiz by just about the distance of the moon. I'm sure other great worriers do though. I'm not the *champion* of worriers but I'm no slouch either. Here's the worry that used to slay me: the magnetic poles reversing. There was so much science talk that it was due to happen. Then in SCIENTIFIC AMERICAN or AMERICAN SCIENTIST, I forget which, I read an article that was the euphoria moment: *the poles haven't been reversing; the continents have moved so much that the magnetic poles apparently reversed.* If that wasn't a feast for thought, I don't know what is. I'm thrilled and happy but faster than a magnetic pole reversal, that theory will change with the next scientist.

When I shared this with my students, it was like a tidal wave crossed the room. Students need profoundly big ideas to balance the necessary reductionist tasks they must do as well. It's like filling the gas tank to take a trip. Feasts for thought define good teaching. "Essential questions" formerly in education vogue have been replaced by "three-part objectives" in my school. Sometimes the programs get rolled out so fast that we never implement them before the next one steamrolls it. Isn't it ironic that the best one was never implemented?

Mihaly Czikzentmihalyi calls this feasting on thought, when people are open and learning like crazy, *flow.* Not quite a rapture, but almost an educational rapture so to speak, when involvement is so thoroughly complete that a sense of time is forgotten. The neurons are connecting and zooming like a Jamaican bobsled team on snow. Flow is the best of all learning conditions.

Lightning doesn't have to strike for blissful learning but a certain hook is necessary. If students are studying celestial bodies in the solar system, they might be asked "can you stand on Jupiter?" This can lead to types of objects in space, types of matter, the meaning of atmosphere and what our anatomy is equipped for. How awesome is knowing that we have another life form right on Earth? A form of life that not only does not require the sun but finds sunlight hostile? These are not just microscopic but full-size creatures that exist on substances poison to the rest of the Earthlings like us. This opens areas of learning such as photosynthesis, chemosynthesis, and the possibilities of life beyond Earth. Good teachers are always subtly doing this.

Rest assured that some jargon-master will claim to have invented the importance of the hook again sooner or later.

Fourth Dimension

"I never saw so many birds before you were my teacher. I'm pretty sure they were always there. There must be other things out there too that I don't see yet. I wonder what they are …."

One of my new fifth grade students said that to me as he came to school early one morning just to do bird-watching with me.

Garish Bulletin Boards

Happy-faced school buses, two-foot yellow pencils with attitude, and notebooks that have musical notes floating out of their lines—all on flexible cardboard splattered on cork, encased, framed wall-type altars with backgrounds of expensive forty-five-inch colored paper. Don't forget the borders in primary colors with more sugary, icons. The frame-like borders are made of a slightly thicker, corrugated cardboard. You could insulate your house with this aggregate of matter. You definitely are cutting down a small tree to accomplish this masterpiece of mediocrity. All this well-meaning commercial preaching obliviously fostered by really nice teachers is a mystery. Kids don't look at it. It's too much to take, most simply look away. This unspeakable schlock is the AntiArt and it's painful. It's an unconscious assault getting in the way of comfortable learning and real art won't stand a chance.

Get a Skill

I feel sorry for the people on personal Jet Ski watercrafts. What are they doing? If not embarrassed by such a display of skill-less, cheap thrills, please reveal the pay-off. Is it the kind of thing you might want to do in some *remote* place where you wouldn't be visible? Can't sail or manage a kayak?

I watched a young person tearing up the high tide line at a beach on the North Shore of Long Island with a dirt bike. The noise was stunning. The loons had just returned for the cold season and this dirt-bike enthusiast was demonstrating something inexplicable. Get a skill instead ....please ....in the name of human survival and education, get a skill instead.

If it is the need to see profound cause and effect, where did we diverge from meaning and "purpose?" Maybe this type of pastime is kind of like the satisfaction of using guns. Even guns require more skill than that.

Am I being judgmental? Heartfelt sorry. Yes. It's a strange path for the living thing with the largest brain.

Contemplating the fun activities occasionally arranged by good schools, ponder the difference between Family UNO Night and Family CHESS Night.

No one disputes the contrasting benefits of basketball vs. digital games. We, at least know what they are. Get a skill ....please.

Getting GOOD at SOMETHING

Endorphins do a quiet rush when a young child learns to tie their shoe-laces. Do you remember when you kept going on a two-wheeler? These quiet but sublime events have impressive results. It's more than a satisfying moment when you actually "think" in another language. After weeks of prac-tice, finally changing chords easily and smoothly on a guitar is an elevated, floaty, "drunk" state of being. It's the strange state of being understated and elevated at the same time:

> − -The process of climbing a tree to a very high level

> − -Sketching an object and the result really pleases you

- -Finally making a great omelet
- -The first time you finally fix something mechanical (e.g. my broken sewing machine)
- -Middle schoolers figuring out how to open their lockers

Success at a specific skill is a profoundly transcendental moment because it's so personal and serene. You're all alone with your advancement in the beautiful privacy of your own head.

Self-motivation is exponentially sacred unless adults kill it.

Grad School Application Biography

For as long as I can remember, I have wanted to be a teacher. An aunt and uncle, who were teachers and had no offspring, took their nieces and nephews to their summer cottage for school vacations. We were city kids and we thought we were in heaven having access to woodlands and beaches. My uncle gave us the gift of physics and geology, and my aunt gave the magic of birds, butterflies, and plants. In addition, since she was morphing from an English teacher to a school librarian, she brought all the books she needed to review. We read and read and offered our opinions. This summer "way of life," climbing trees, identifying shells, learning to swim and dive, and really getting to know authors was indeed idyllic, and we knew it. We were too far from good television broadcasting, so in the evenings, we took walks, played ball, put fireflies in jars, identified constellations, looked for Sputnik, and read. It was a very academic setting, but we didn't know it. It was a culture, a very breezy, easy, authentic way to learn. One fact built upon another, or we didn't learn it. We were energetically self-motivated, thinking about a new project for the next day, but not worrying about being idle, because something interesting always presented itself. Let's build a chipmunk trap! Let's turn the wagon into a go-cart. Let's count the barnacles on the rock. We learned to write letters home and to our friends who were either home or at summer camps. Although these letters were obviously crafted by children, they were genuine communication.

I was a successful student and went off to college as a Secondary Ed French major. I placed into such a high level French class that I was overwhelmed and received a grade of "C" my first semester. Without any emotion, I matter-of-factly transferred to Elementary Education with great curiosity. A few wonderful professors later, I was certain that the pure form of learning I experienced during the summer as a child could be replicated as an instructive way to spend a day.

As an elementary, middle school, pre-school teacher, and college instructor, I believe my greatest accomplishment is in the promotion of a content-rich curriculum. Promoting a dynamic curriculum that is tinkered with every day and capitalizes on what the day has to offer is the consummate task. Fearing a workbook-driven curriculum for my own children, I founded a small private, nonprofit school, Sprout House, Inc. in Chatham, NJ. There was no such thing as "gifted," or learning disabled, or special ed., because the hands-on component was so strong. Kids actually liked coming to school in the morning to work on their projects, prepare for frequent field trips or whatever they felt like they needed. Learning to read and do math was natural and pleasant, but ancillary.

After fifteen years, I felt compelled to move on to the greater challenges of urban education. Believing that teambuilding helps a school enormously, I organized a number of successful retreats for teachers to bond socially and intellectually. In addition, we invited support staff, (custodians participated) to join us.

Afterschool and Saturday clubs were projects I worked very hard on. It included a drama/poetry club, and a science/field trip club. In addition, a coworker had the idea that if we met on the same night as PTA, attendance would increase. This was indeed the case. The first three years, I did this as a volunteer. The fourth year, the science club was a paid position. Many more years of after school clubs have transpired, some years paid, most unpaid. The years of volunteering to lead a number of clubs, I have listed as accomplishments, but could also be seen as community service.

During the summer of 2004, another teacher and I decided that the "schoolyard" was such an ugly, miserably hot, stark place that we spent weeks of our vacation, designing and painting a mural.

As far as community involvement, I try to attend weekend rallies for different causes.

I developed two gardens at our middle school   with my colleague. One is a courtyard with trees and plantings and outdoor benches and rustic decorations. The other is an urban meadow near the entrance. I also spend time with former students gardening at the school in the summer. Additionally, I try to make time to take former students to the Newark Museum, NJPAC, and other venues on occasion, after school.

Emphasizing the message that most of every day should be spent doing real things (such as gardening, bird-watching, studying terrariums with invertebrates, discussing current events, doing action research, community service, planting seeds, building structures, doing experiments, acting out skits, reciting poetry, cooking, fundraising, studying the weather, creating art, music, developing physical skills, looking at history, gathering stream study data, etc.), those real things should be evident every day. When the notion of representing knowledge in codes (of words and math) becomes bigger than the content-learning itself, we stop making sense. We wouldn't, as adults, be asked to deliver a written document on the subjects with which we had limited familiarity. It follows that children might feel less inclined to symbolize subjects before they have mastery. Authorship is a profound experience and school sometimes bullies children into this experience.

Confounded by the struggles of some of my middle school students to write sentences and solve word problems in math, I transferred to teach in an elementary school. I will offer two anecdotes that should illuminate the situation: 1. My class and I were doing our math one day in September when the classroom door opened and the math "specialist" in the building entered and announced, "I will be teaching the lesson every week at this time." In that one period, she conducted a lesson on: area of a rectangle, the perimeter of a rectangle, the volume of a rectangular prism, the circumference of a circle, and the area of a circle. She lectured loudly at my fifth graders and spoke quickly. 2. My fifth grade class was next door to a first grade class. Early on in the year, I heard a commotion through the wall. My prep period had just started so I went next door to see if I could help the teacher. One little boy was scowling at the teacher and doing a combination of talking and crying.

I stood there in case anyone else in the class needed anything. I noticed that they had their journal-notebooks open. One student was finishing the last letters of her name. Other kids were making random letters on random lines and to my amazement, a little girl was just making squiggly forms perfectly on the first line. The teacher, with whom I was starting to become friendly, told me the mandate was "first grade must write ten sentences a day in their journals." These stunning moments make it urgent to examine what kids are enduring in schools.

Grandma (and perhaps Mr. Trump)

Grandma, did you ever imagine that your lace runners would live in the same house and the same linen closet as your daughter-in-law's embroidered pillowcases that her mom made in Sicily as a girl? Also sharing the linen closet, the grandson-in-law's Romanian tablecloths from his family's flight, precious enough to drag along. Sometimes side by side on the holiday table, the differences in Quebecois and English handicrafts are complements to each other. Did the makers of these fine techniques, in all their contemplative hours, know that as the threads would grow softer, they would be in the company of such captivating diversity? The African sculptures and the Irish linens are housemates passed down in this humble real estate, like American children in a classroom. It's an interesting development, Grandma, and we like its distilled, but understated, charming effect.

Guilt

Student absenteeism is the teachers' fault. That would be absenteeism worthy of state-mandated repetition of the school year. Sixteen absences and you repeat the grade. More than half of my students have sixteen absences by May. That becomes my fault (and students **rarely** repeat a grade for that offense), and additionally, students with poor attendance have trouble passing the test used to evaluate me.

The administrators hound the teachers to stand in the hallway when classes change, to keep students from exuberantly running and jumping (or worse). But **many** administrators don't stand in the hallway EVER. I dutifully stood in the hallway for years, but now it's too dangerous. I can get broken bones too.

The administrators hound teachers to change attendance rosters electronically when an "absent" student comes very late and therefore turns into a "tardy" student. But we're not allowed to sit down or do anything but interact with students. I agree with the interaction part and I don't want to lose class management to stop every time the door opens and a tardy student walks in, because it's not a rare occurrence. So sometimes I forget to change the attendance before lunchtime. To solve this problem of teachers being so overwhelmed about classroom management issues to change the roster, the administrators have added another layer to deal with. Now we have to do hard copy paper work in addition to the electronic records to send to the office by lunch time, whether or not we have neglected to change it electronically. This is a brilliant move to tick off the box, showing that the administration did something to solve the problem. They're redeemed. The teachers are once again guilty.

The teachers need to leave five days' worth of lesson plans in their own absence folder (in the main office) and enough copies for all students. I have more than a hundred students so that's 500+ pieces of paper in my file. But wait, the period is eighty-four minutes long, so I need two activities. That's now 1000+ pieces of paper. It gets better; the lessons need to be current, so I need to change this file constantly. Any administrator knows this system is more breakdown than function. The administrator has dictated the plan and copied it to the super. The teachers are always left holding the pieces.

This happens for almost every problem that arises—administrators come up with a plan and teachers must implement it. Administrators are good to go. That is until they learn right from wrong and admit what's really going on.

Helping to Homeschool My Grandson

My grandson might be in about third grade now if he were in school. I spend time with him doing the horizontal and vertical curriculum. Sometimes we have a huge, integrated macro-experience, such as a day trip to Sandy Hook, NJ, to experience an environment with a lighthouse, dunes, seals, whales, waterfowl, birds, snails, crabs, fish, plants, and maybe a snowy owl *in winter*. We try to swallow up the whole thing with all the parts. We try to put the parts together without pressure as he picks and chooses things that interest him. Then we try to visit the history of what the place felt like back in time. This, of course, continues back at home for a few days later, maybe longer. We try to visit places in other seasons as well or twice in one season or twice in different conditions. We always make time to play in situ (digging in the sand, climbing trees, etc.).

Sometimes homeschooling is just about the vertical curriculum—a worksheet on fractions, Venn diagrams, and/or learning about simple machines. The vertical curriculum can be totally random or connected to something. We need to think about covering the basics. The funny thing is it's never random in the end. He always connects it to something he knows.

He is a sponge who is a walking computer. He remembers everything and applies it sooner or later. I rely on him for information. It's a fun way to live in my retirement from full-time work. I never thought of this existence, but it found me.

Right now my grandson's challenge is writing. He's not very interested in things his mother and I suggest. His counterparts in real school can write up a hurricane, I'm sure. He resists until he thinks of someone he wants to communicate with. Spelling might also be a challenge since it's really not an organic exercise. He's a strong reader, but he will get another chance at spelling drill when he wants to learn cursive writing.

I always tell my graduate students that decoding is a natural human endeavor. Encoding is a profound experience for when you are experienced and mature enough to want to tell the world something.

Homeschooling can be a way to decode your world.

High School

I've never taught at the high school level, but I've spent a lot of time in those buildings for meetings and workshops. If nursery schools are imbued with ingenuity, high schools are suffused with hilarity. As a teen, I remember floating around in a state of silly contentment. How many minutes go by without a joke coming from somewhere? Not many. If any jokes were at someone's expense, it did not seem to be anything but disguised endearment. I was blessed with wonderful teachers and extraordinary friendships. FYI, I was not in the in crowd, either.

I'm sure my positive experience was just luck and my own children might have had very different experiences. I've heard some stories that are troubling, past and present, but my friends and my teachers were sweet, present, and comical. Going to dances, parties, ice-skating, the beach, ski club, and sports was paid for with babysitting money. We had dances every weekend. Is that why we were so well-behaved?

At the high school level, I can't think of anything more important than helping science and social studies researchers, by working with SciStarter. This is a citizen science nonprofit enterprise in which ordinary people gather data for researchers in thousands of different ways. You might be counting tadpoles or trash items in a park. Data is submitted on an online platform. It can be done from anywhere. For older teens and young adults, Earthwatch, a service -travel organization, asks you to work with scientists in the field. Although it costs you money to do this, I was lucky enough to have the Dodge Foundation pay my way. I studied and protected the seaweed–snail–crab–gull food chain on an island off the coast of Maine. Opportunities are offered worldwide.

I have no professional experience with high schools but omitting any mention of such a profound part of life seems negligent.

History Class

As an adult past middle age, I am reading Tony Horwitz's *A Voyage Long and Strange* and Roxanne Dunbar Ortiz's *An Indigenous People's History of the United States.* There is no history book or lesson, in my education as a child or undergrad that was accurate. Grand and wondrous, White-European American Origin Stories are not just gloss in seventh chords. They are robustly counterfactual. You can't steal, torture, kill, and drag children from parents and then put a rich, highly developed fancy bow on it. So many mindsets now need to be reacquired.

The afterbirth has arrived.

History ….All the History

When you really know a subject and you see that subject published, you may be amazed at how far from accuracy the concepts may stray. So as a child, you go from no notion of history to forced consumption of a mere *slice* of the whole story. Consider African American children who are subjected to living in a culture where only European American lines are traced and texted as if there were no context. As these lines are described, in the example of American history, we know that the great potential of this new society was made possible by the slavery of non-voluntary immigrants. Almost all industries in the North and South were directly or indirectly nourished by the brutality of slavery. There is therefore a double insult—no mention of your heritage—and the omission of how your ancestors fostered and promoted the comfort and success of other people *at your/their own expense.* If a child is numb to this sin of omission, a state of bewilderment might be manifest. If a child is wise to the black hole of heritage, rightful anger is an expectation to these self-respecting individuals. It goes without saying that Native American children are subjected to even worse insults from the sanctioned atrocities.

On a completely different complaint of how history is taught, consider the omission of "place-based" learning. Children should know the stories of the nearby land and landmarks, despite whether it includes their cultural background. How did indigenous people take advantage of the topography?

Did they exploit the land or live wisely? Students should know what dinosaurs lived in their neighborhood. They should know how the adjacent rivers contributed to primal peoples' and conquering people's economies. Older children should understand the word "exploitation" in regard to the past and present. They should know to what other continent they were previously attached. NJ was attached to Africa at least one time. That gives students a sense of how truly gripping a powerful history is. When it touches you in some way, you remember it.

HORIZONTAL Curriculum Is Always There

A. There are two ways to think about curriculum:

- Learning things in depth with thorough attention to connectedness is the Horizontal Curriculum.

- Lockstep progression is the Vertical Curriculum.

Everyone needs both.

B. The horizontal curriculum is always there. Just turn ten degrees in any direction and you will see something new to learn. You could also call it learning a "system." The comprehension of a system involves embedded understanding so that when something goes out of equilibrium, you can troubleshoot easily.

C. When most people learn things in a vacuum, it is hard to retain that information. Seeing the information in action and in a setting allows the learner to use the information which provides the possibility of retention and a good chance of being able to apply the new knowledge in a variety of situations.

D. The Horizontal Curriculum (HC) is doing fun stuff without realizing that you are learning; the Vertical Curriculum (VC) is the "no-nonsense," serious business of targeting a skill or skill set in a predetermined list.

VC Example

Changing a Tire:

Vertical Curriculum Flat tire Fixing—

1. Gather jack, lug wrench, spare tire
2. Collect the owner's manual
3. Apply the parking brake
4. Apply wheel wedges
5. Remove the hubcap/wheel coverage
6. Loosen the lug nuts
7. Place the jack under the vehicle
8. Raise the vehicle with the jack
9. Unscrew the lug nuts
10. Remove the flat tire
11. Mount the spare tire on the lug bolts
12. Tighten the lug nuts by hand
13. Lower the vehicle and tighten the lug nuts again
14. Lower the vehicle completely
15. Replace the hubcap
16. Stow the equipment
17. Check the pressure in the spare tire
18. Take your flat tire to a technician

   Alternatively, a person could spend the day with the Triple A worker as she goes around fixing flat tires. This would be the Horizontal Curriculum way to learn the skill.

E. Think about where VC comes from. Someone has mastered something and wants to help others in the most direct way without absorbing it organically. VC is a blessing; HC is authentic.

How Do Kids Learn to Read?

When a kid has a burning interest in something and a thoughtful adult realizes it and finds a thick, all-inclusive catalog on the subject, it's better than Christmas. They will learn to read with this wrinkled treasure within a few days. ***Really*** learn to read.

It Can Happen

I am a no-nonsense teacher until boundaries are FIRMLY in place. With some classes, the evidence of my good sense of humor never allowed the students a fair education. They thought they were at the playground. I did them a disservice and vowed there would be no repeat performances the subsequent years, at least until we hit our stride, academically.

One year, a difficult female, sixth grade student, did not want to do homework, which happened to be meaningful, short, and sweet. She preferred socializing to attending our science lesson. I called her mother one night. With obvious distress and compassion for me in her voice, her mom said, "I know she's difficult, but she's saying you are a racist." After my blood pressure normalized and a sleepless night, I went to the principal the next morning to relate the incident. The principal said, "I know; a *different mother* called yesterday to relate the information. Evidently the mother of the child doesn't believe it, but told this other person." The principal went on to say she had to "process" the claim with the superintendent. "You *know I* don't believe it, of course." Later that day when I had the class again, four random students were removed from my class for questioning. I was later told the results to the question, "Does Ms. White ever say or do anything inappropriate?" One student said, "Yes" and gave a wild story, which contradicted itself at many turns (I was not told this lavish story). The three other students made strange faces with knitted eyebrows while slowly saying "No." The principal closed the case and told the super not to even bother with an interview with me. However a lot of damage had already been done in the community. As a teacher who always worked nine or ten hours a day, spent so many Saturdays and summer vacation days in the neighborhood painting murals, gardening, joining marches, running (volunteering) family field trips and more, this wasn't just emotionally crushing, it temporarily made me physically ill for about a day and half. Why aren't "my people" (hundred plus students per year generates many awesome family friends) speaking up for me? For some reason, I managed to rally, despite lack of support, and insisted the student be transferred to another science class. The remaining nine months of the school year were uneventful in that regard.

Fast forward a year. It is again early September, and one class (first period) decides to disobey a school rule en masse. I try to work it out with them, but can't figure out why they are doing this. I matter-of-factly assign detention as mandated. A parent asks for a conference. I require the guidance counselor to sit in. The violation is covered briefly and then the mom asks, "Are you a racist? It's a discussion in the neighborhood."

I say, "No, of course not," and I look at the counselor and say, "I think it would be best if 'Alisha' were transferred to the other class."

"NO WAY!" the mom says, "I liked what I heard in your class on open school night. I want her in YOUR class. I like the activities in your class. I do NOT want her transferred."

Someday the nuances will make more sense. "Alisha" and I had only respectful, informative, and genuine interactions from then on. It could have turned out fundamentally different. All this because one kid didn't want to do easy homework a year before. They're just kids trying to make sense of the world. I was lucky.

In the First Place

Technology advocates rail on about how technology and the internet transform your classrooms into genuine temples of learning. All the prescribed benefits should have been in place with great teaching: relevant materials, challenging levels, and lots of motivation or, better yet, self-motivation.

As cool as technology is, it is no different from the debut of the print-ing press or long playing records, very cool ....but the wisdom of education comes and goes to a better place. When that other technology taught humans to "encode" things, education became a different animal but the systems or layers of information needed and still need to be rich and meaningful. Before "encoding," processing of information had to be satisfying digestion. It wouldn't work otherwise. There was no place to put it except in a brain cell. Now that we can "encode," facts and systems can be put on a shelf while the next facts can be trundled in and experienced superficially or authentically for long periods of time.

The delivery is all jazzed up now. Jazz is good but if it is not digested slowly and savored, it may be fleeting.

It's All About Saving Our Adult Butts for …. Standardized Test Scores

"Go to this workshop."

"Do it this way."

"Now do it a different way."

"Do yet another boring, gaggy, writing project that the kids can't relate to."

"We have to get the state off our backs."

"This will increase their scores."

"You must finish that math chapter and move on!"

Yeah, it increases their scores for *this* spring but by the time September rolls around, we find that these practices have not ensured that they retain the information. The result is that the adults are scot-free but the kids still suffer from not being scholarly, informed, or even competent if we can talk about urban challenges.

I know firsthand because my middle school students are very shaky on multiplication facts, sentence structure, and basic punctuation. Math "word problems" were almost futile. To puzzle out why this was happening, I transferred to the fifth grade in the elementary school and saw how the state bullies, with weak, flimsy, superficial pedagogy. The state, in turn, is of course bullied by George Bush's No Child Left Behind and Obama's Race to the Top. In my urban district, it looks like a state of overwhelm. Worrying about and monitoring what is going on in the percentage of rooms with substitute teachers is gut wrenching. After that, what's left of this human being, the teacher, could be laziness or insulation for sanity that *appears* as laziness. In the case of true laziness, it's all about saving adults, not about serving children. Ultimately, the threat declares that after six years (in the old days) without much progress, adults will lose jobs. The threat is presented to make it about adults, so adults, being survivors, do anything they need to do to superficially remedy the situation. No Child Left Behind came and went and morphed just as umpteen other programs have come and gone in my forty-plus-year career as a classroom teacher, and we still, more or less, herd young humans into a space with thirty five square feet each, and move symbols around all day no matter how young they are, or how lost they are.

It Looks like Trauma

The sixth grade lunch is troubling. The noise level produces a strange suffocating feeling. I have been hurt twice in one year during lunch duty. The first time, I was circulating and chatting with kids. As I walked between the lunch tables, a student jumped up, the top of her head hitting me under the chin and her foot coming down so hard on my shin that I buckled and fell. Her launch was like an Olympic sport. My tongue was bleeding, my gums were bleeding, and my nose was bleeding. Other kids and the girl herself picked me up. I was a mess. I was lead to the nurse's office leaving a trail of blood. The girl herself was "just playing." Her only intention was to run around the cafeteria. She is a sweet kid and she was apologizing over and over.

On another occasion, I was standing and talking to a student when I was hit by a backpack sliding fast along the floor. I was knocked off my feet. Luckily, I bumped into someone (who didn't get hurt), to break my fall to the floor a bit. Backpack-sliding is a sport similar to curling ….I guess.

Anchor charts: Teachers who are compliant with the number of anchor charts in their classrooms have created an environment that looks like a house of someone with a serious mental disorder. Homemade charts of quick facts from floor to ceiling. This is my nightmare. Even genuinely therapeutic settings are intentionally serene and not like that at all.

Rubrics: Rubrics were created by the oddly challenged people for reasons that appear slightly deranged. Don't try to parse them or you will become mentally ill. At one time, and maybe even now, an individual rubric evaluation was required as a part of every graded piece of work.

All this looks like trauma to me.

It's the Economy, Smartie

I am riding my bike on a cool summer morning before 8 a.m. through the park woods. It's a serotonin-filled pastime. I can even do it without coffee. The beauty of it all is absolutely a religious experience. Spider webs are revealed like no other time of day. I see a little wood frog, a fat monarch caterpillar, a praying mantis too close to the road, a deer sticking its head out of the grass as if in a storybook, and the crickets are still playing a tiny background melody. It's dreamy and wonderful but I am a goofy outsider all blissful; I am looking at a scene where all the individuals are part of a seriously fierce economy. It's all business for them and cake for me. It strikes me so in the morning more than any other time of day when everyone is alert for an opportunity as light provides one more important sense, vision. Of course, the book *Freakonomics*, by Stephen Dubner and Steven Levitt, has changed the way I think about everything economically. It's not a bad thing; it's the fair and just thing.

I am a suburban woman entering an urban school setting everyday as the goofy outsider. I have no real idea of the swath of gut issues with which pubescent kids come to school. I am guessing they're focused on what is being socially networked, their amorous thoughts, their clothes, and shoes, and their weekend, for starters. Like being in the awesome woodland, my students are cute, funny, entertaining, and adorable but this adult, hard as I might try, doesn't know for sure how everything fits together for them and if they truly even give schoolwork much serious space in their economy, if it's even possible to stay alive socially if you devote too much time to schoolwork in the scope of things. One of my student's family was selected for the reality TV show where the house got an overblown makeover. After the show, his fingerprints were found on the fire alarm after a false-alarm event caused us to vacate the building in winter during midterms. He was a really good kid. Another social economy anecdote involves a backstage interview with a choice of NJ Nets players. I got this prize (for a chosen student) for simply being a good patron buying a subscription of school newspapers at the time, around 2005. The deserving student was thrilled but I knew to keep it very quiet. When he came back to school the next day, I asked him how it was and he looked at the floor and through his teeth said, "Later." I made a mistake making an overture during school hours. When good things happen, the interpretations can spread in unexpected exponential directions.

On a scale of 1–10, does school even show up on an adolescent rating? I don't know and I doubt if the psychologist-experts do either.

When I finish a school day with my students, I don't feel the need to walk in the woods; oddly, I feel invigorated by their interest in science and all their academic energy but I don't know what's really going on in their providence, as they produce and consume ideas and facts.

Janitor in the Penn State Locker Room

The janitor heard and saw a horrible scene in the locker room. He didn't tell any authority because he was afraid he would lose his job. I feel like I might lose my lunch at that comment and then I think about how I am given the choice of following a damaging curriculum or risk taking the "intervention" that needs to be done. If caught, straying from the script, a teacher will find himself on a "sixty-day improvement plan." This particular curriculum is probably no different from any aligned with national standards. It is a program that is a confusing, impenetrable, glutinous, dense yawn. The non-science teachers in my building could not pass the first quiz. This script is forced on me to present to the sixth graders and I could lose my job if I don't. The creators of the script don't know my students, our topography, weather, animals, plants, fungi, local history, or our challenges. They sell a pretty package that is generic and that's insulting. I know the impact it has on kids' brains. I know the impact it has on their unconscious attitude toward school. Failing in school affects a kid's life so dramatically. It's not the trauma of the Penn State locker room, but the dreadful effects are mostly permanent. Everyone makes their own decisions. I'm not proud of mine.

K–8 Schools

A year or two ago, I was so tickled to hear that the old-fashioned K–8 grade type school might be resurrected. I went to a K–8 neighborhood school in Brooklyn, NY, in the 1950s. Was it perfect? Probably not, but I liked it and flourished from time to time. I remember that a few weeks after my mom had a baby, a paraprofessional came to my classroom and said, "Your little sister needs you," and they took me to her first grade classroom. She was weeping and said she didn't know why. I talked to her and held her hand until she stopped. I think it only took a few minutes. I don't know how *I* felt, but I knew she felt a little better. There are lots of people in city neighborhoods, but there are more opportunities to stay connected in neighborhood schools. Older students supervise younger ones before school and I was able to help my sister in this kind of natural setting.

K–8 schools offer fewer opportunities for hormonal drama with fewer adolescents in one building.

Older children take pride in being the models.

Please spare me the argument that middle schools have specialized equipment like labs. Just get it **if** you're really using it.

While we're at it, let's ditch the departmental classes until after eighth grade, especially in troubled schools. Find teachers who aren't afraid to teach all the subjects and truly work with a class like all great fifth grade teachers. The key is finding great teachers. Greatness can be identified and others can be mentored. We'd be no worse off and everyone would feel attached to their group/class and no one would be running the hallways. Having 200–800 adolescents (age from eleven to fourteen) in one building is just too much hormone production in one place.

Level the Playing Field

Corporate charters and for-profits (FP) remove students for a variety of reasons a few weeks or so after enrolling. How do I know? Because I get them back in my class in throngs. I continually ask guidance departments if they track this data since they must now worship test data. Not so much. Corporate charters and FPs don't expel students. They just make life so miserable that difficult students don't go back.

Charters and FPs teach until 4 p.m. Monday through Friday, Saturday mornings, and various hours during the month of July. Students don't realize that when they apply. Those schools pride themselves on their strict rules. It soon becomes tedious for students who don't have good coping skills. The students withdraw and try to catch up back in the public school curriculum for which they have missed content. The low scores of those students contribute to the dismal totals of the public school. The scores for the charters reflect the scholars who are benefitting from the rigor.

Lockers And So Much More

Many experts in education have written that a sense of mastery of specific or general skills has a tremendous effect on the general positive outlook of a student. Successful acquisition of proficiencies fosters intellection motivation.

The first week of a middle school career has many elements. The most important is, "Where is my locker and when do I get to use it?" It's a claim to a space in which you have complete control. You can decorate it. It's a solid, metaphoric root. It says you are an official middle schooler, with babyish grade school behind you. Learning how to open a combination lock is an additional sublime sense of mastery and has all the satisfaction of cracking a code. About five out of a homeroom of twenty can read the directions and quickly open and close their little dominion. Those five will help five more with success. The other half of the class will persevere and with a few more tries on their own, five more will succeed. The last five may have fine motor difficulties or will develop frustration because too many things can go wrong. If you go past the number slightly or don't go far enough, the combination won't work. If you get confused by right/left directions or if you have a habit of rushing through activities or have difficulty with a *list* of directions that can't be broken down individually, success will be a challenge. The instant the "click" happens and the door swings open, the happiness and relief on the part of the student is like radioactive energy. There are smiles, sighs, words of affirmation, and relaxed tension in the neck, shoulder, and hands. It's a remarkable surge of endorphins for such a humble activity. "Locker graduation" is big! We need much more respect and study on this unique phenomenon.

The "high" will last for a certain amount of time. If interesting activities and challenges are presented in the window of all that self-respect, there will be greater chances of accomplishing more skills. The dendrites and terminal fibers are still stretching and pumping. If locker-happiness is in a vacuum, however, the power of mastery will diminish with time.

I stopped doing "class rules," the syllabus, goals, and other b-word* activities on the first day of school. Since the past few years, I go straight to the science "grabbers." I usually launch right into microscope use. Each student gets interesting objects and slides, different from one another, and then they must write about what they see and write the directions on how to use a microscope. Students are busy working and sharing with each other. They must get the message that the euphoric "locker-type moment" can persist alone and/or with the help of others.

* boring

Lockstep Progressions

Virtual schools worship at the altar of lockstep learning and so do I. I take no credit; John Dewey, Jean Piaget, and many others have taught us that any material can be mastered if you take smaller and smaller baby bites and if necessary, vomit it back up, rinse out and take another taste. In the late 70's, I worked in a school where at 12:45 p.m., every adult in the building took a small group and, eight grades turned into many more reading levels. No matter what grade you were in, you went to your reading-level class. Virtual learning takes it a step further. You alone are in your group. The acquisition of skills is up to you. You have complete control of your language arts or math destiny! Staying in that class and not necessarily moving on is also a powerful motivator if there are no disabilities. If public education could pull this off *without* crushing the complementary hands-on learning, a wide range of children would progress . . . smooth as silk.

A modified, or different approach is needed for diverse learners.

Virtual schools are, in fact, very upsetting to me, but this aspect of it is worth a look.

Looks Like Electrons Moving: Blue Ribbon or Failing Schools Alike

At the risk of over-generalizing, Blue Ribbon schools are sometimes negatively characterized by slouching (and baseball caps lowered over glazed eyes). Students in low-scoring schools are eager to see what the teacher has in store for the day, ask detailed, ascending questions, and make genuine eye contact. One of the challenges of failing schools is the muddiness of the behavior range. Most days are totally enjoyable in a hands-on environment for teacher and students. However, occasional trouble can occur. Teachers get interrupted, pens get stolen, books get tossed out the window, lockers get pummeled, teachers get interrupted, notebooks get ripped, homework is sketchy, tests are ignored, fire drills are disrespected, attendance is poor, students are without pencils/books, and did I say teachers get interrupted? Hallway behavior is complex. The problems trigger more problems. Parents come without appointments and stand in the doorway, expecting the teacher to stop mid-sentence and have a conference. Teachers usually **do** stop when this happens because they want to see the parent badly. Silliness springs in as the teacher turns his back to talk to the parent. Behavior is so complex that the majority of teachers do not have engaging lessons; filling in the blanks and Smartboard programmed clickers predominate as learning activities and therefore it's easier to accommodate random interruptions. The school becomes a venue for health screenings, so classes are interrupted sometimes without notice, for the doctors, nurses, and dentists. This can happen during a lab session, final exam, review session, leaving for a field trip, assembly session, special program session, etc. That's the negative end of the range. The positive parts of low scoring schools are many, too. This miraculously includes high interest and readiness to learn. Bright, beaming faces don't pretend to be disinterested. Probing questions demand attention to one's specific developmental level. There is no fear to ask a question. There is a robust desire to learn. The world is their oyster.

When everything reverts to looking like electrons, protons, neutrons, quarks, etc., there is a cosmic overlay as the energy takes on a life of its own. The rhythm of the energy has a pattern—and why not, we're part of the universe just doing what astrophysics does and water rolls downhill.

Lost

You're a sixth grader; it's one of the first days of school in September. The math teacher is introducing quadratic equations. You're still fuzzy on the seven times table. Your mind goes into liquid Jell O. Do you: a) act out to cause a distraction, b) keep writing anything, c) put your head on the desk, d) suck your thumb?

You're a first grader in a new classroom that's not kindergarten. You have a brand-new writing notebook and a new pencil. Your teacher calls the notebook "a journal" and tells you to fill the whole page with writing. "Write about what you did yesterday or write about the story we read yesterday." You know you can't write so: a) you fill the page with little wiggly lines, b) you fill the page with letters you know, c) you hit the kid next to you, or d) you get out of your seat and do what you want.

A self-respecting kid has many options, many of which are listed above. I have seen all manifestations of this scenario. It's all too common. Contemplate how this plays out when it's a never-ending proposition.

Lunch

The lunch periods are probably too long (forty-three minutes) because the cafeteria truly looks bizarre. There are at <u>least</u> ten out of 200 students who are always out of their seats, and who could blame them? The remaining 190 are hunched over their trays, arms protectively preventing the tray from being snatched, and feet are entwined in bookbag straps on the floor. The provokers are either poking unsuspecting people who are trying to eat, lunging but not striking, or really sucker punching someone. Add to this, merciless cutting in the lunch line and people who jump up, steal a lunch, and throw it. Oddly, there are only a few food fights, because I think punishment is quite severe. Book bags are thrown or slide by on the floor. Once in a while someone stands right on the table. Last but not least is the pounding. Sometime something is going to break. There's <u>very</u> loud pounding on tables, walls, seats, etc. It's not cool drumming; it's just pounding.

I was hurt three times in one year of middle school cafeteria duty, which was only on alternating days. I got in the way. I just got in the way ....nothing personal. We are not listening to what we are being told.

Marriage and Sharing

The offspring of relatively stable households think of our parents, and other people's parents, as unquestionable institutions in themselves. When I met my future parents-in-law, I saw them as a mighty piece of bedrock. But when I heard their backstory many years later, I realized that all serious, older couples were just flaky young adults flung together with gossamer. They grow together and mesh their idiosyncrasies into formal idiosyncrasies. That's the underpinning of civilization growing, in some cases exponentially. Hopefully "permanent" coupling is the right mixture of similar backgrounds and different backgrounds. It's hard to form a new mini-institution if there is no overlap at all, but the doldrums could set in if there is too much overlap. Not exactly a case for arranged marriages but a serious thought. No overlap means there is going to be a steep learning curve, which if embraced, can work. Marriage is not all glamour, as you realize, ten years in, paying bills together and possibly thinking of an old flame. It is the rapture-test to pay bills together for twenty years and still get all giddy when you hear the other car pull in the driveway. You have schlepped together and slept together so if it's great . . . it's **great.**

When people just work together, at their day-job (or are on a volunteer committee together, or fundraise together, or serve on a board of directors together), and share workloads and resources, they are figuratively thrown together with anywhere from zero overlap of ideas and backgrounds to fully counterpoint backgrounds and perspectives. The good "sharers" will stand out if they see a glimmer of responsiveness in others, even without merit rewards, especially without merit rewards. They will do it for the benefit of the group and the project. They will become a bona fide, mini-institution in themselves. Conversely, when I hear people say, "Alex is an awesome person/friend," my answer is, "Let me work (share) on a project with her. There's a difference. We'll see!"

Good sharers can turn others into good sharers. It can be contagious. Think back to your best moments. Giving or receiving, it's all good for schools. It's the only thing that works.

Master Teacher and the Script(ure)

When I made the transition from authentic teaching to urban pseudo-teaching, I came with twenty-nine years of successful classroom experience, founder of two small private "authentic" schools, and twelve years as an adjunct professor of pedagogy. Nonetheless, I was forced to readjust to the expectation of a "fill in the blanks" mentality. Few read my resume after the initial hiring, probably because they were spending so much time putting out fires, understandably. The principal and assistant principal recognized my abilities, but in a failing school, a great steamroller program is adopted by a subject area "leader" and no one alters it. No feedback is requested and unsolicited feedback gets no response. There is therefore conclusively no reason in the world to attract good teachers to failing schools. I watched and waited. My observations gave me ideas for short and long term fixes. I wanted to roll my sleeves up and do what needed to be done. No way. The sacred script is handed to the teacher: new teachers, poor teachers, great teachers, mediocre teachers. End of story. Why is there a movement to even attract good teachers?

The master "career teacher" finds himself with the weight of two options. When the tests and practice tests are delivered week after week, cycle after cycle, and the kids' eyes fill up at the sight of them, he might tuck them in a nice closet and go outside instead and release the butterflies that need to migrate to good flowers as scheduled because a storm is predicted the following day. This also has the added impact of fraudulently reporting the scores that don't exist. Conversely, the decision can be made to obediently drop what the teacher and kids have worked so hard for, and spend the morning with a test from a stranger, always fostering behavior drama. Again, it's hard to understand why there is any need for a teacher beyond robot capabilities.

Matt Ridley's Evolution of Everything

Matt Ridley's new book *The Evolution of Everything* maintains that all systems exercise a constant striving to work better and better. I love this idea. I love this idea except for the field that I am most experienced in—education. One enormously grim idea after another has bullied children ever since they have been corralled in rooms to become skilled at one thing and another. The good ideas are out there and have been out there forever. Why doesn't anyone promote them on a large scale? It's because the education industrial complex can't be changed easily. The education gurus at the state level have far less experience than me and yet I must adhere to their demands. These would be, for the most part, "for-profit" oriented demands from the kingdoms of Pearson and Microsoft.

Here are some successful systems:

- We have seen that rural summer sleepaway camp sometimes helps kids flourish.
- We have seen that fishing with your grandparent provides enormous academic underpinnings.
- We have seen that "college" is a more agreeable arrangement for learning than many elementary or high school frameworks, probably because it offers choices.
- We have seen environmental education changes mindsets and offers uplifting experiences.
- We have seen that kids learn more in clubs than they do during the school day.
- We have seen that public libraries make their communities excel in countless ways.
- We have seen how certain senior-living communities are a good fit as far as intellectual stimulation and happiness.

With all these great models, it's curious to see that our children are subjected to the mediocrity of being in "desks" too much. We need to see our youth in systems that provide better ways to grow and develop. Schools are not evolving.

Sustain the Image

Class photos from the past bring more joy than you'd think. Viewing pictures of beloved teachers and friends provides a sense of not losing a part of yourself. If things were "good", seeing old pics promotes integrity. Little children should always have these available, good or less than good….last year's teacher and friends, a former nanny and a grandpa who lives a great distance. Older children will find a sense of lightness and stimulation at the same time when these items are accessible. Sustain the image.

Middle School Prep

Nothing is better prep for teaching middle school than teaching in early childhood. In early childhood, children are scanning the environment for interesting things and teachers need to offer a world with a wide variety of options. Middle schoolers need that even more. We provide learning choices for preschoolers, and middle-schoolers need skillful adults to do the same. Recognizing the social interactions as factual info is acquired is important in both age groups. Delivering those opportunities is critical. Knowing the mini steps in fact-acquisition is intriguingly similar. We break everything down in early childhood and we should be doing that with twelve-year-olds too. Both groups are very buoyant in disposition, reactions, and searching-propensities compared to the slightly more contemplative elementary school kids.

No one thinks twice about offering learning centers to nursery schoolers, but are notably startled at the sight, in middle school.

The way we look at young children for creativity, joy, and diligence is the way we might be looking at young teens.

We look at the whole child in early childhood, and have an academically overweight focus instead, for the older group.

Misbehavior

Misbehavior occurs when a percentage of teachers in a school building have shaky skills. Of those, half are shaky because their brains are fried from the relentless confusion of changing programs, systems, analyses, and reports. The other half doesn't have the skill of mind-reading, creativity, and desire to do lots of work. It's a self-preservation thing. Kids know when teachers are not up to it and they act up, even if unconsciously.

Misbehavior occurs when you only come to school four days a week and you're lost and can't catch up.

Misbehavior creeps in when you've been disappointed too much (the bus doesn't show up for the field trip, a program fizzles, computers don't work, a teacher takes a leave of absence, etc.).

Misbehavior is constant when a teacher is too controllingly strict or too easy and friendly.

Misbehavior is exponentially predictable as class size increases.

Misbehavior is rampant when you're over your head academically.

Misbehavior gushes when people treat you in confusing and hurtful ways, especially when you're very young.

Misbehavior takes effect when the previous teacher rewards you with candy.

Misbehavior is what self-respecting individuals project when something is really wrong.

It's a cosmic communiqué.

(And Even) Mosquitos Are Different Now

Even as recently as the '80s, kids played outside without fear of ticks. Mosquitos were not as prohibitive to our activities as they are now. My offspring were children of the '80s and they were fortunate enough to be thickly enmeshed in the outdoor world. Having to say "outdoor" world is ironic in itself. "Indoor" world should be the exclusionary phrase. They tore up leaves and pretended to cook with them. They dug in the soil. They mashed a flower or two to make "paint." Shrubs were for hiding, fireflies were for jars, and pine needles were green beans.

Raw materials were abundantly available to us and I was a city kid! Today we worry about the environment. We worry about manicured yards. People live on the tenth floor. Parks are not for tearing up.

Call me crazy but if you watch kids like I do, you will notice a primeval oneness with the way children approach these natural materials. It's definitely at the expense of the natural materials but it appears very purposeful and automatic. Clay cakes and chicken wood were favorite activities of my children. Using a discarded baking pan our "soil" contained mostly very fine particles and they stuck together nicely when baked in the hot sun. It was hard to resist when garnished with dandelions. An old log could be shredded nicely into what was known at our house as "chicken wood." *Hours were spent on these activities,* literally.

As a teacher, a favorite field trip of mine is to visit a stream. Clean streams usually involve cobbles or pebbles or somewhat flattened stones. One activity is to take dip nets and find invertebrates. Another is to allow random play. Nine out of ten times, the children reinvent the engineering of the stream with the rock material. They create channels, pools, waterfalls, and rapids. They race leaves or sticks. They usually cooperate or divide up and find a new location. After all, streams are not finite, or at least they shouldn't be.

We're hitting a turning point where it feels like the planet might be getting back at us in an anthropomorphic way. Even peanuts have turned against us, as evidenced by their utter prohibition in classrooms. What's next? The red flags are everywhere. Delicate ecological balances shift and we suffer with red tide, masses of stinging jellyfish and-the great trifecta of floods, tornadoes and garbage patches to name a few. It makes the old testament look tame.

Much More than an Overtone

My first child was six months old when I got the call requesting me to take an adjunct position in the education department at Kean University (then Kean College, old Newark State College). Long before she was even born, I did not know how I could put a child into the education system of day-long workbook pages sitting in a desk. This was more than an overtone; it was a deep, profound ache. Even worse, I had no control over my nieces and nephews, and friends' children, and the ache, I was afraid, might turn into an emotional or physical ulcer. It's hard to explain how much I just could not let this happen. Mediocrity/boredom was such a painful notion and no one in my social circles homeschooled then.

So I took the adjunct-offer phone call seriously. Although not directly relevant to my problem, I knew there would be some help to calm my throbbing brain. I would be gone for three and a half hours two nights a week, so it did not affect breastfeeding too much. This was the push I needed. Wonderful colleagues supported the crazy idea of starting a school (mainly Marge Kelly and June Handler). "Just do it" was what I heard them say. Years before, when I was a graduate student, Lillian Peters told me that my crazy idea should be manifested. She identified me as a career teacher, and even called me up at home before the baby was born to suggest a sophisticated pediatrician that I could tolerate. "Joanne, you know you're driven." She died before Sprout House opened; loved that woman, Catherine Dorsey Gaines and Mimi Vogel too. I don't know if Sprout House would have happened without that graduate school circle. Kean was such an awesome place as it was smaller and unpretentious. The instructors worked so much magic for me. In order to be in a graduate program, a weekend orientation class was required in the woods. Rocco LaRusso offered it and I can't even remember what department the "class" was in. I was probably in my late twenties and felt so uplifted by the diversity and the sheer amount of science I came away with and the people skills that were unconsciously embedded. " Living" in the information and walking the walk prepared me for Sprout House where I hope it transferred. I also signed up for a few field trips offered by Mike Searson. He made it look **effortless** to rent two passenger vans, drive to "The Village" (NYC) and hear Maurice Sendak talk in a small venue room of a NY Public library. Field trips were now permanently on my radar.

My husband, Larry, and I spent so much time studying nature in simple and nearby beautiful places that he was immediately taken by the idea to open a private school (or at least he acted the part).

Aunt Grace and Uncle Mike gave me $2000 (this was 1984), and my deep workbook-fearing ache started materializing into Sprout House.

Multiple Choice: Lots of Wrong Answers in Your Face

It changes every year in my school but more often than not, the emphasis, if not the edict, is to use multiple choice questions. They can look the usual way or be more creative with long answer–scenario options.

It's not a secret that multiple choice is the mandate because it's practice for the state tests, clear and simple.

The child has perhaps learned some facts, gets to the test, ponders whether it is a trick question or not, ponders some more, then chooses an answer. All that pondering with the wrong answers in your face is enough to mix up your brain. Incorrect materials (the wrong answers) are thoroughly embedded like soup. I have seen children who can apply factual info before the test, but a month later have lost it. Their last experience with the material was the test. Do you want a surgeon who was trained with multiple choice tests?

My Tiny Hope

My hope is that my students will be walking along a sidewalk in a modest neighborhood in late spring and see an evergreen tree. Every single one of them will notice the pale-colored new growth on the ends of every branch screaming out the announcement, "Look at how much I've grown this year." My students will walk over and quietly, but contemplatively, examine the needles and remark, "Oh, much better than last year, but not as good as the year before." In this pipedream of all-encompassing science/math concepts, those students who are constrained by life's problems will be no different than the luckier ones, because of their immersion in the real world.

Mother Could Tell

My mother could tell the weather from a short glance at the clouds.

My memory thinks it was 100% of the time whenever we needed to care about the weather. It was a morning thing, but she also predicted in the afternoon with stunning accuracy. She and her six siblings were born in this country, but one of her grandfathers was an extremely successful Sicilian farmer. He was so successful, that he was commissioned by the government of Mexico to develop figs, olives, and dates. He lived there for seven years and my mother's mother was born there.

So some sensorimotor intelligence was floating in my mother's neurons, or she picked it up from the brief amount of time she had before she lost her mom at age seven. Maybe this effortless knowledge was passed through much older siblings, if indeed this weather forecasting skill came from a farming perspective at all. I tend to think it did, but maybe she picked it up on her own.

Skills are picked up and absorbed from everywhere.

Myths, Omissions, and Lies

Myths, omissions, and lies from our '50s' and '60s' childhood textbooks are even more pernicious, pervasive, and overarching than initially suspected. This unbearable, leaden, slow, realization reminds us how smoothly we drank the Kool-Aid. Taking for granted, an American "way of life," as humane, moral, and even exemplary, it is the acid reflux of emotions when the creepiness apparently self-manifests as truth. When it feels like nothing could be worse than the Thanksgiving myths, American Discovery stories, empty frontiers, etc., along comes industrial practices forcing domestic animals into cruel situations, all the while promoting cute farming scenarios, the wonders of Disneyland with public transportation terminals just out of reach of undesired neighborhoods, and the seizing of Hawaii. It wasn't even *spin*, just old-fashioned lies. If the fact that slavery built the nation's economy was obvious, Redlining, of the Roosevelt era was a secret. It's a heartbreaking mess of a delusional dream. We're not "that" glorious nation worthy of the 7th chords in our stirring patriotic songs since we can't even condemn torture anymore, liberty aside. What would Henrietta Lax suggest for a social studies syllabus? Even the strong and "adventurous" Vikings had enough sense to back off when they identified 3 distinct cultures in the new land. It was a no-brainer to them. Icelandic museums thoroughly and easily offer this in overt and obvious depictions. Recently, I hiked along the cliffs in Ditch Plains in Montauk, NY, which is only a hundred miles from where I read textbooks as a child. I just learned that after the Spanish–American War, our African American soldiers were sent on the train to Montauk, then walked a great distance to where Shadmoor State Park is now. They were forced to quarantine or die from Malaria in that location. That wasn't in my childhood textbook, although the Spanish–American War was. It's all easy to condemn from my living room couch. It's all so complicated as evidenced by seeing that even someone as conscionable as a recent President, fell into a rough spot too.

The Review

In my twenties, and more specifically, just after graduating college, I made the tough choice of working at a ski lodge in Quebec over substitute teaching in NJ (since there were NO teaching jobs.) Ha ha, tough choice! We skied (downhill or cross country) Monday to Friday from eleven to three, cooked breakfast and dinner for fifty-five, washed toilets, and vacuumed. On the weekends, we changed linens and checked people in and out. We partied many evenings a week in a wholesome way, which included dancing to local bands.

I have visited Mt. Sutton about every ten years since then. To this day, I still have dreams, which include the actual trails on the ski slopes which tell me at least two things about brain activity. Experiences are a matrix of overlapping actions. Large interwoven concepts are more powerful than isolated facts. Those trails are so strongly influencing that they become metaphors in unrelated current dream experiences. I'll be skiing down a specific trail and end up in the school cafeteria, or ride a certain chair lift and end up in my aunt's kitchen having a serious conversation. The second neuron-integrity notion is that the ten-year review of the trails, despite the infrequency, is also very powerful. The "review" process couldn't be more convincing.

NEWSLETTER (Sprout House)

April 2006

Dear Parents,

How old will your children be in the year 2030? Your grandchildren? Every day is Earth Day around Sprout House, so we have never made one day stand above the others or one teacher's style of reverence dominate. It's always a good thing to receive gentle criticism on a habit that might be Earth-destructive. Don't be shy; just be gentle and helpful. We try hard. Lists abound on things to change even in our home-lives which do all add up (and might break the spell on consumption ….). If we all made a commitment to tinker with one

Earth-friendly habit like fewer plane rides or clothesline drying, it might make the predictions of atmospheric imbalances for 2030 more merciful. But it's getting so late; we're on the greenhouse express. Please remember to list your wildlife sightings.

Night Before the Evaluation

I have the pressure of the world on me tonight because I have a formal evaluation tomorrow in my sixth grade science class. It will only be for twenty minutes. There are probably eighty criteria points. The gimmick du jour is, "Let them (students) collaborate and teach themselves and teach each other." Every good teacher has known this forever. But in an eighty-four-minute class, the collaboration portion might have come and gone by the time the evaluator gets there. The evaluator might show up for the clarification of any misunderstandings. You will then lose a great quantity of points for the dirty word "lecturing." On the other hand, you will lose points if you have not shown data that you actually DO the clarifications. You are constantly required to hit both ends of a spectrum and therefore can be demonized for not doing the opposite style. If you are doing "multiple response strategy", the evaluation will say….."the teacher did not offer individual response strategy". If you are doing "data analysis", the evaluation will say…."the teacher must practice Language arts literacy approaches". If you are doing math calculations, the evaluation will say…"the teacher must demonstrate a hands-on approach."

When the evaluator just gets it wrong. "The teacher must use anchor charts." Anchor charts are small, teacher-made, concept-type posters. I used "meteoroid, meteorite, meteor with pictures and definitions," " mass, gram, paper clip," "lunar MONTH in phases (all twenty-eight plus), and "planet sequence and Origin of the Solar system." I was downgraded for lack of them. They were there in plain sight. I have no recourse because it's their "cutting and pasting" word against yours. It's come to dated and timed photographs of classroom settings to prove the evaluator has made a mistake.

Evaluations demonstrate the science of "gotcha."

No Teacher Required

Getting back mini-evaluations, called "walkthroughs" and formal evaluations, I know that teachers are no longer allowed to teach. Students must teach themselves in collaboration with each other. I have been guilty of direct instruction many times.

This gimmick du jour is something I actually agree with but not ***exclusively***. My science students should be outside identifying all the plant species in a square yard. They should be using homemade weather instruments to assess the momentary conditions. They should be using microscopes to describe our soil structure. They should also be scrutinizing the movie *The Martian* for any science errors or exaggerations.

But to give students, and especially students who are not honor students, a dry, eye-glazing excerpt, article, or Smartboard presentation, and tell them to construct some knowledge of their own, even in groups, is appalling.

"Direct Instruction" is a curse word. Avoid being caught at it even though it might only be for a moment. As much as I agree with that sentiment, there are times when I **really** want to ***w.a.l.k.*** my students through a concept, regardless of their learning style, because it only takes a few minutes. I don't want them to see it print at first . . . *because* it is *so* confusing. For example, when teaching (teaching is a dirty word because implies direct lecture) the concept of lightning, I don't want them to see the whole concept at once. I want the cloud with mixed positive and negative charges to stand alone for a minute. Then I want to show the increasing condensation to cause the negative charges to sink down and separate from the positive, as I draw it on the board step by step, giving them a chance to slowly copy it. Then we look at the charges in the ground rearranging themselves because of what's going on in the clouds, again drawing it very slowly. And so on . . . until the results make perfect sense. Stopping for questions allows necessary interaction as well.

Haven't I been trained to explain by breaking down concepts until the struggling learner is finally at his or her own exact level? Isn't that supposed to be my greatest skill? My superlative craft should be in sublime explanations! Now it isn't anymore.

Not Rats

Winding my way on the second-most curvy highway known to humans, the Southern State Parkway, along the south shore of my beloved Long Island, I always grip the steering wheel with two hands at positions 10:00 and 2:00. This highway was built by Robert Moses to be somewhat scenic as it delivered white people to the suburbs and beaches. It was meant to be driven at forty-five to fifty miles per hour. Only the Northern State Parkway is curvier. For sure, in nearby Connecticut, the Merritt Parkway, a parkway sibling, is very similar.

My husband is nodding off next to me when traffic slows on this summer Sunday evening. I am creeping along the western edge of Suffolk County coming close to the border of Nassau County. Now I am barely creeping. I secretly enjoy this situation because I can identify tree species and even wild-flowers. At points, I am even stopped with only short advances. During this private, personal wildflower observation-session, I recoil in horror because I see a rat in the median . . . and another . . . and another. Whatttttttt? I look at my husband blissfully asleep. I can't wake him. I look back at the median and the sun is catching light on leaves or something. No, it's ears! Those mammals are *bunnies.* For miles and miles, anywhere there is shrubbery and a ten-foot strip of grass in the median, there are oodles of bunnies. This phenomenon continues into Nassau County. My husband is still asleep. No one will believe this so I am tempted to wake him, but someone's rage-horn honking does it for me. Now, of course, we see nothing. "Keep looking," I mutter. He sees one . . . then the whole three-ring circus is on display. Whew! By the time we get to JFK airport, we are wondering if we both were dreaming. We were not.

The next day, I tell my seven-year-old grandson, that I have a story for him. When I do this, he is eager to hear and he *knows* it's going to be a crazy nature story. This is the revelation for me. We tell each other so many crazy, biblical nature stories. When are we going to realize that these phenomena are not miracles but occurrences that happen regularly around our human-made societies?

The two of us ponder the many possibilities that could have caused this, including storm drain highways too small for predators, etc. We think hard about whether the situation will continue indefinitely or crash. My grandson looks up to the left; he looks up to the right. Left brain, right brain . . . it doesn't matter. The emergent curriculum doesn't get any better than this. It never fails to probe the best thinking. He's got many hypotheses.

Reflection Essay *NUTRITION AND THE TEACHING AND LEARNING PROCESS March 31 and April 1, 2007, excerpt*

In 1986, I founded a small private school, Sprout House, Inc. in Chatham, NJ. It served grade six down through nursery school and summer camp. The whole idea was to showcase the fact that school should be a multi-faceted concept. This model demonstrated how children's days should be spent learning about the world, living in a society, and being happy and healthy. Food was a big part of the curriculum. We went outside for fresh air, exercise, and learning everyday above 20 degrees Fahrenheit. We gardened, we baked wheat bread every Thursday, we made homemade wheat pasta and created different types of flour muffins, etc. Children participated in and studied all the food. Since food is a big part of life, I believe that we should know where it all comes from and see the beauty in it. I have since moved on, but Sprout House is still happily planting sprouts, etc. I was very pleased to see a course that addresses this issue and spreads the message. The course confirms my beliefs that fruits and vegetables are beautiful and delicious and they need to be promoted in school. At Sprout House, children did not bring lunch *because* we wanted to make a point about healthful eating. Many of the parents, especially ones with allergic children, chose the school for this reason (among others). The other parents chose us for other reasons and considered us food-Nazis. That hurt. On Halloween this year, I brought apples, yogurt, organic peanut butter, and granola to my urban fifth grade classroom. I let my students spread peanut butter or yogurt on flat cut pieces of apple, and sprinkle granola on top. My students were very happy about doing this and they ate a lot. During our cycle test schedule, I served cream cheese on flat leaves of red cabbage. All but one student asked for more, lots more. On another occasion,

I spread hummus on the red cabbage leaves. Again I got lots of enthusiasm. I never expected this but one child asked if he could bring fruit for me to cut up for the class. It has become an institution. Almost every week, someone donates a fruit or vegetable snack for the class. This outcome was unexpected.

According to our text, Roberta Larson Duyff's <u>Complete Food and Nutrition Guide,</u> natural sugars and processed sugars have been around for a time. Sugar processing promoted slavery in the Caribbean; second, it harmed the teeth of European aristocracy, then the health of common people. Intentionally or unintentionally, it keeps people temporarily happy as it boosts serotonin levels. It is cheap enough to eat as frequently as the next "rush" is desired. It keeps people in a rut (my non-empirical observation). I teach in an Abbott district and I watch kids take handfuls of candy from their pockets after school. The addictive nature of sugar has crippling long term effects relative to degenerative disease. Because of the huge quantities consumed by some families, they suffer more immediately from obesity and diabetes. The mother of one of my students has an enlarged eyeball. This grim situation is a symptom of diabetes. It has spiraling implications, because her son, my student, is now exhibiting out-of-control behavior, which I believe is related to worrying about his mom. He actually talks to me about her condition.

The same behavioral phenomenon follows with chip-type, processed packaged snacks. These food products are cheaper than real food, and they contain large amounts of salts, possible trans fats, hydrogenated oils, etc. Again, this is a <u>staple</u> in many neighborhoods; the trash on the sidewalk next to the school at 9:01 a.m. is the evidence. It's swept, and then appears again at 3:15. Before this class, I did not have a grasp on label-reading, because I don't eat many packaged "foods." Now, when I pick up a wrapper, I read the label. Especially instructive was the revelation about the trans fat fractions below "1," being allowed to print "0!"

References to junk food in school settings, I think, miss the point of a wholesome, thoughtful education. Junk food fundraisers will be outlawed in NJ, but posters and decorations that glorify sugary or processed food are a mixed, if not poor, message for children and teenagers. Those subtle reminders could easily trigger the craving cycle.

In the last segment of class, Susan asked us to share nutrition challenges in the classroom. I made a comment that I feel is the entire heart and soul of the matter. One person responded in a way that reveals that they missed my point or didn't hear it correctly for whatever reason. A part of me thinks that teachers don't want to hear it or simply can't grasp it. I was emphasizing the fact that giving students <u>any</u> external reward debilitates the hope of internalizing the pleasures of learning. Deep, innovative teaching addresses the whole child and his/her attitudes and propensities for lifelong learning. Habits of eating (1) and intense curiosity about learning (2) are the bottom line. When my students are busting down the door to get in, in the morning, to check on their experiments, terrariums, write a letter to a politician, sing a certain song, write a poem about a blue jay, or get some new spelling words, I would be ashamed to disrespect them and treat them like jumping seals at Seaworld by rewarding them with a treat. I think they would be insulted as well. Did it happen overnight? No. They came from classes where they were given candy for behavior, long book reports, and doing A or B+ test scores. Excuse me, but isn't A or B+ a reward in itself?

I am always looking for meaningful math applications for my students to ponder and calculate. When they can't relate to word problems they are at a disadvantage. So much of their years in school have been reading about other communities from national textbooks or calculating things that they can't understand. I came away from this class with all kinds of ideas to utilize real math. Already this week, they have calculated their BMI and BMR. That went over so well that they made calculations on their parents too. Since pH numbers are exponents, we have calculated that math as well as crossing over to the science curriculum. I took photos of the sidewalk outside our window for three days at 9:01 and 3:01. I enlarged them, printed them on copy paper, and drew a scientists' type grid over it. Each student got a quadrant to count the trash wrappers. We did all kinds of calculations with this. *They did this much more enthusiastically than they do textbook math.* Then they came to their own sobering health conclusions. I made up some math problems with actual products, that I see kids eat, to calculate possible trans fat. This is *perfect* for our study of fractions and percent. I didn't try this one yet because I am still making them.

I have been more or less ostracized by colleagues for my policies about fostering healthful lifestyles that I needed a course like this to simply feel normal. I try <u>hard</u> to mind my own business, be humble, and not be accusatory. Even the teachers that feel a certain appreciation for good nutrition will still give the students a bag of candy at holiday time and bring them Dunkin' Donuts on a field trip. I found out that the music teacher who has my students' first period every morning has been giving them candy before 9:30 if they do what she wants. She confessed to me and told me she wouldn't do it anymore. (She was really nice about it and didn't even know how I felt.) It's lonely out there. Even with a pending NJ law, I doubt if there will be any enforcement with so many other problems in my district. The week before the NJASK test, the math supervisor made a special trip to each classroom to tell the students to get plenty of rest and not drink any extra water the mornings of the test. When she left the room, I had to contradict her. I said, "Ms. L was mistaken. It's important that you drink water and I am going to have water for you in the classroom. You do get bathroom breaks, but she was concerned that you would need to go more often. I know that you will have no problem waiting for the breaks." My Basics Skills teacher was noticeably irritated that I gave them water and she tried to take it away as I distributed it before the test. I can't wait to get my UFO ball and have her help with the activity.

With my own offspring (two adult girls), I never bought junk and never even gave them anything to drink but water. Because juices just start babies on the sweet-craving, I gave them fruit, but only water to drink at home. However, I also never made it "forbidden fruit," when grandparents and neighbors gave them a treat. This is an area when I do feel health-conscious parents go overboard to rudeness. That's just my opinion!

My (baby boomers) generation is probably the generation with by far the most people who were never breastfed. That leaves us with a health handicap. We were also the generation that was raised on the new sensation of fluffy, squishy, nutritionless Wonder Bread, steady amounts of canned and frozen vegetables, and the birth of food products to promote corporations. These two factors are alarming when you think of the other four million years of *Homo sapiens* history with human milk for babies and real food. The next twenty years of geriatric outcomes will be very revealing for this particular generation.

All the materials in this course have given me current documentation to promote better health. This is enormously helpful to me in politely trying to change my administration's policies. Because I wasn't nutrition-current, never calculated BMI or BMR, etc., and learned so many new things that are still sinking in, the class enables me to show all the sides of valuable leadership. There isn't space to comment on exercise which completes the circularity. I have been nominated for "Teacher of the Year" in my school, to compete further. "Healthful practices" is a big part of my message.

Duyff, R.L. (2002). *Complete Food and Nutrition Guide.* Hoboken: John Wiley & Sons.

Kennedy, R. (2007). *Addiction to Sugar* The Doctors' Medical Library. net/sites/_sugar_addiction.html

Renwick, E (1976) *Sugar History* Retrieved April 6, 2007 from *Let's Try Real Food*, http:www.sugaraddict.com/Sugar_History.html

Oregano Is "Just a Weed"

In my sloppy, happy, playful, experimental, haphazard gardening, I put oregano into a pot on the deck. My mother loved "orrrhdehgano" and used it in everything. Who knew it was a weed.? To her, it was spun gold. At my now ripe, old, sophisticated number, I learned oregano is a weed. The seeds of the plant happily spill over the side of the deck in the wind. I was walking next to the deck and got an intoxicating whiff. I walked back . Another blast. I looked down and there it was—a beautiful shag carpet just sweetly outgassing.

These are the special moments. In teaching, it's plumbing the environment for every learning experience possible. The closer it is, the deeper the cognitive effect. Study everything that can possibly reach the senses. The learning will last and be used and then applied to totally different situations. That's not just good academics; it's creativity.

Did I mention that oregano comes back year after year (if the conditions are right)?

P.S. Regretfully, oregano is not native to N.J.

Over-Generalist

I have some other kind of intelligence. I don't discuss novels, although I love reading great ones. I can't discuss anthropology, although I am madly in love with Australopithecus (and *Homo habilis*). I can't discuss geology, although I was relieved that the electromagnetic poles are not switching (there's a theory that it's just the tectonic plates moving around). I can find monarch butterfly eggs in the wild, watch them hatch into caterpillars, molt five times, make a chrysalis and transform, but I am unable to discuss molecular biology for very long. I can throw a pot, but can't choose the right glaze by myself; play a guitar, but reading music is very slow. And most importantly of all, I can't discuss multi-celled life in outer space without giving a stern lecture about the Vent Life right here under Earth's Oceans.

I am cursed by being a generalist.

A generalist. Yes, good teachers, especially elementary school teachers should know that being a generalist *is their specialty.* Being able to see the connections that cross the curriculum is a gift or something that can be developed very enjoyably. Try *anything you're interested in* and let it lead you. That interest will go from one unexpected place to another. It's the beauty of a matrix, fully threaded to cover large football fields or small whims like water in capillary action, thorough and sure. Students who lose track of time and space because they are engrossed in something systemic and intricate are building neurological frameworks. Teachers should be similarly absorbed for their own sake and to be emulated by kids.

I love the idea of bicycle mechanics, especially as an afterschool club, but I am dismal at car mechanics.

That could be next on the list.

Play Is the Matrix

We've known for a long time that nothing is more important than play for adults and most profoundly for children. NOTHING. Watch children in the most desperate of situations and they manage to be playful unless they have been pathologically traumatized. There's something to it folks. Why do we ignore it?

At Sprout House, I used to joke that we called it recess when we came *IN* the building. We are so lucky to have large open spaces, fields, black top and woods to experience and explore. Then, oh my gosh, we visited a new and interesting habitat (meadows, rock formations, streams, etc.) for the ultimate playful pleasure in addition to the lesson. This happened on average one to four times a month.

The exuberant behavior of a middle school hallway is searching for time to play. Running, jumping, joyfully swiping, and kicking each other looks like bedlam but it's a serious overture. And not just for physical education. They have that. Self-motivated playful tinkering, swinging, ball throwing, jumping, climbing, etc. are needed but get squashed when neighborhoods are too dangerous. The confounding, silly behavior of a middle school cafeteria is also a scream for play.

EVERYTHING builds on a playful foundation. Neurons branch in a healthy way when the learning is self-actualized. There are so many master-pieces written on "play" the genius activity of human history that it is not necessary for a rehash here. Watch a child carefully climb a tree for the testing of principles in physics or wolf cubs tumbling around on top of each other as they are magically, unconsciously learning to hunt and the matrix of play will reveal itself. A quiet but sublime feeling of satisfaction is evident. It's not evident after ten lockers in a row are scratched with something metal or when the red EXIT sign is punched in a handsome, dancelike leap. That result is more like happy hilarity.

If you lose yourself in a positive way, you're probably playing. Look for it.

(I'm Not)Playin'

A lot has been written. We've known for decades that life without play can be pathological at worst and very questionable at best. In urban America, parents think twice before they let their kids outside alone. In a large school building, it's not a surprise then to see kids bursting through the hallways, slapping signs, and making a jump shot for the ceiling tiles. That's what self-respecting creatures do. They take matters into their own hands.

Pulling Off a New Business

Pulling off a new business or a new project is monumental. Pulling off a new enterprise with a six-month-old strapped to your chest is how scar tissue forms. You don't notice it happening. The strength comes not from magic but from human infrastructure. Frameworks that are unconsciously a part of you. My consistently even-tempered, cheerful, fun father balanced my mother's genuine loving, but sometimes hysterical, temperament. My aunt and uncle's summer science cottage was a living diagram for a school. My network of awesome siblings and cousins, aunts and uncles was a warm, dazzling circus.

My husband and two daughters have sternly, lovingly, and humorously created a home where awesome ideas are constantly funneling in. It's unconscious and on "auto." I think we're spoiled.

There is also the luxury of friends who taught me things without either party knowing it.

You just take them all in your pocket, like money that never dries up.

That's how you start a new enterprise …you take it all with you, not in a greedy way, but in the backdrop of honor… from former couplings to the entire network around you. The truth is good or marginal; you take it all. Human infrastructure and communication in general, is the best part of learning.

Quirky Days

What about the days when a teacher is not at the top of their game? I tinker enough that hopefully there are not many of them, *if any.* But still, things happen, and imperfect things might only even be someone else's perspective. Our childhood memories have incidents that felt lousy but were not intentional on the part of the adult leader or teacher. We can't dwell on it but we can't forget it either. One adult to fifteen or twenty-five students will render a "miss" now and then. Hopefully, we are forgiven. In many cases, we don't even know it happened. We hear, "That's life! They'll get over it," but toughening up little lives should be minimal. Teachers need to be aware and guard against it because everyone has a different take on any action.

Randomness and the Sweet Spot of Mediocrity

Australopithecus had all together crummy teeth, fur, claws, strength, speed, and probably climbing ability compared to other animals. So it had to rely on outsmarting predators and prey. Random brain energy "on steroids" was a powerful thing. It might have even triggered consciousness. Same with the very vulnerable shell-less octopus ancestor.

Conversely, the luck of a planet being in the perfect orbit of its star, shape-wise and distance-wise, the amount of material that stayed stuck together and became rocks, not gases, the lucky crash-causing tilt, and the crash-induced, sizable moon, rendering tides, reveals the *upside* of randomness.

The teacher who isn't formidable at anything but likes everything can become the striving Australopithecus or the lucky planet for her students.

Reality

My dentist does beautiful work. I know this because the endodontist remarked about it to his assistant while treating me. His comments were detailed, showing how truly impressed he was. I would love to be free to just do great work with the same satisfying sense of accomplishment, simply helping students in thorough and productive ways. An honest day's work with problem solving and mastery and the psychological space to deliver it. That would promote the profession and ensure honest learning experiences.

Refraction or Diffraction

I haven't been there in ten years, but I used to go every year and, in fact, lived there once for six months. In winter snow, especially, the woods and mountains of Quebec, not too far from civilization, is a remarkably quiet little town. It only takes six minutes after you leave the center of town, and you're in wonderland. It just has its way. One crystal clear, snowy, exquisite winter morning, I noticed that the large paper ("white") birch trees were each a different pastel color. Peach, pink, yellow, turquoise, greenish colors. Wait, something is just refracting. (Or is that diffracting?) This is crazy. Only the large, fifteen-plus-inch diameter ones were doing it. No one else was around. Why didn't I see it before when I lived there? It can't be the Monet effect, because each tree wasn't shy about its own color. It must have been more about the angle of the light. Whatever it was/is, I have seen it again and again mostly at the very top from a privileged chairlift, I confess, and riding solo. It makes me think about when children tell me capricious stories and how I react.

Resiliency

I am two weeks away from some kind of retirement. I figured by now that I would soften and regret my decision. But the hell never stops amid the joys. The confusion ramps up as it always does in June. The 1:30 p.m. spring concert (for which I had to cancel a biologist's visit for a special lab) is still not happening at 1:45. Normally, each grade would be called in ten-minute intervals thirty minutes prior. No communication—email or otherwise. Message from the teacher next door: she's just teaching because she hasn't heard anything. Are parents showing up downstairs in the auditorium? Parents who have taken off from work? A security guard tells me the music teacher is absent. The music teacher is of course the concert coordinator. Now I am wondering if they will reschedule on the day I have rescheduled the biologist's visit. I am thinking about all this while I teach the contingency lesson, the physics of cold fronts.

A few years ago, a principal needed me to sign some papers that *he* had forgotten about and barked on the PA system for me to come to the main office immediately and that a substitute teacher was covering my class. This was the last hour of the last day of the year. I didn't get to say goodbye to my class and never gave them the little science presents I had for them. I had no warning. "Luckily" that was a self-contained fifth grade classroom, not a hundred kids.

Everyone has come to school dressed for a Stream Study. The nets, buckets, field guides, charts, and instruments are ready on the sidewalk. We are on the sidewalk too. The bus bill was never paid or processed. We return to class for the day.

The kids have experience with random school chaos and disappointment.

Now spotlight the joys—every year, I have over a hundred students. It's intriguing how different everyone is from each other, because teens and preteens all try to be alike. There are so many different finely chiseled traits. Surprises wait around every corner. If traits were assigned colors and shapes, and a mathematical rendering could be formatted graphically into a matrix, I am sure I would be dazzled by each design before me. Not as interesting as the people themselves, but surprising and beautiful. How does disappointment manifest itself in your personhood/personality? How do the mediocre teachers who can't pull off anything but boring classes (so they often add candy and somewhat inappropriate music), factor into a student's psyche? The resiliency is astonishing; not unlike the obvious resiliency found by historic and current survivors of physical and emotional brutality? I'm sure the results are sometimes manifested in unlikely ways. So I pick up the pieces and hope that most pieces can go back together in unique and interesting ways. Resiliency is an artform.

Respect For All Teaching Styles

Although I am proudly in the camp of "high-engagement, content-rich, and authentic experiences," I have great respect for every possible teaching style being able to captivate and appeal to learners and learning. I have seen various individuals employing enough clever humor to lectures that ninety minutes feels like a blink in time and the facts are digested thoroughly and satisfyingly. All my whining about the gimmick approach could prove wrong with the teacher who can make it work. The point is that once the goal is agreed upon, a person should be able to create a path to the finish line, maybe with the exception of a scared novice, because a year or more of straightforward, unobstructed learning is mind blowing. Your own successful power-recipe is your creation. Invigorating best practice can be truly a shuffled deck of cards.

REVERY (and Divine Strategies)

To make a prairie. it takes a clover and one bee,
One clover and a bee,
And revery.
The revery alone will do,
If bees are few.

—Emily Dickinson

A magical occurrence that master teachers experience is the phenomenon of materials and ideas funneling at you exactly when you need them. You don't like what is suggested for a science lab and you're riding your bike and see some discarded junk on the street that would be a perfect alternative or just triggers a great idea. You need a certain "hook" for a complicated lesson and voila, you hear an idea on National Public Radio. You want a supporting poem to go with a science or social studies lesson and a friend offers an unsolicited idea. A troubling local news item underscores a concept in civics class. This stunning actuality happens more and more as teachers "click." More than a coincidence, I call this elevated state of being "divine strategies" or "the unfolding." You bump into things you need with a spiritual urgency. It's a kind of mental magnetism. When activities go south, a phoenix humbly arises. It's when skill and confidence are earned and the individual knows how to plumb the environment and appreciate all sweet and unpretentious elements waiting to be rearranged effortlessly. It's all out there, so I guess this blessed equanimity is just the skill of achieving heightened filters and deferential wonder.

Rewards

A pure and transcendental school setting would be 1.engaging, 2. relevant, and 3. productive. Engagement is a no-brainer. All that youthful energy enduring crappy, boring, soporific question-and-answer learning is probably being sucked out of our atmosphere into a cosmic substance, probably the origin of dark matter and dark energy. It's beyond belief that that much energy can be squashed day after day in millions of schools around the planet. Interest levels need to improve. Beyond being interesting, the subject matter must be relevant for each particular group of students. Tailoring is another mandate. The disregard for productivity in schools is also unbelievable. Most kids are spinning their wheels, running in place, not accomplishing things for anyone, including themselves. They could and should be doing baseline research of anything and everything, creating history brochures for their neighborhoods, volunteering at meaningful projects, creating pop-up shops and more.

When these three things aren't happening, teachers get desperate. They resort to artificial rewards. This is the most profound disrespect for children and teens. It screams, "You're not learning or behaving, so I'm going to treat you like a dancing seal." Something is very wrong with the system if something as wonderful as learning, luxurious old *learning*, needs a reward. It also screams, "I can't teach."

I was a fifth grade teacher receiving students from a fourth grade teacher, whom I will call Mr. Peabody. He had a system of distributing "Peabody Money" every week to well-behaved students. They could use their money to buy out of homework or select a toy from the "incentive shelf." It's hard to create a transcendental learning environment when you follow that act. The students got it (my learning goals) and appreciated it on some level, but they were confused for a variety of reasons. I think they were stunned that there were no rewards in my class. Then there's candy, donuts, pizza parties, Chinese food rewards, etc. The class across the hall can smell it. In my urban middle school, I've had students miss exams because they were partying with another class. Is sugar a way to keep the masses down or is it just lazy teaching? It's not the first time or the first era in history that "power-holders" used treats to lull and quiet the noisemakers.

I also concede that once that steamrolling mindset takes over a school, even the good teachers have trouble dealing with it and just give in.

Rocks Make Life and Life Makes Rocks

The beach I played on as a child had (and still has) a 200-foot bluff behind a stretch of pebbles and sand. Sometimes erosion caused clay to puddle at the foot of the bluff. I remember stopping short at the sight of the clay puddle, and I wasn't the only kid to be thrilled at the sight. We would take our sneakers off in a flash, add more water to the puddle if necessary, and slide in. Our brains went to an alternate, euphoric place, as we were mesmerized by the sensuality of skating barefoot in the clay. It was an unmistakable altered state.

As scientists now know that minerals combined with organic compounds to create the first life, clay is the material that really shows how all its surfaces allow elements to attach to it.

The metaphor is not lost in the classroom. Every subtle nuance of information can and should be interesting and complex for each child to react to in their own way.

Keep it organic. Keep it integrated.

Rubrics 1

Element Superhero	Score 4	Score 3	Score 2	Score 1
Introduction of the Element/ Writing	The main idea is well developed, using important details about element, family, and correct physical properties. The topic is thoroughly developed and incorporates creative story.	The main idea is reasonably clear. The information is accurate about the chosen element and physical properties. The topic and story are developed but not complete.	The main idea is not clearly indicated. Some information is inaccurate or missing. The chosen element is supported with few details, and is sketchy and incomplete.	The main idea is not evident. The information given about the chosen element is not supported with details. Story is not supportive of element and missing physical properties.
Design of Atom/ Subatomic Particles/ Labeling	The main design of the atom is well developed, all subatomic particles are shown and labeled correctly.	The main design of the atom shows accurate information, all subatomic particles are clearly shown but not clearly labeled.	The main design of the atom is present. Some information may be inaccurate or missing.	The atom is not clearly designed. The information shown is not correct or relevant to the chosen element.
List of Physical Properties of Family and Element	The correct physical properties are listed according to the chosen element. The information is accurate and impressive.	The correct physical properties are listed according to the chosen element. The information may lack details.	The physical properties of the chosen element are listed. Details may be missing or inaccurate.	The physical properties may not be relevant to the chosen element. Information given may not be present, accurate, or supportive.
Element name/Atomic Mass/ Symbol	The element's information is accurate and included all required information. The information is clearly shown and impressive.	The element's information is accurate and includes all required information. The information may not be clear or creative.	The element's information may be missing, unclear, or slightly inaccurate.	The element's information may not be accurate or missing.

Rubrics 2

Micro-managed scoring means the scorer can't be trusted to guide a "learner." If teaching required consummate, highly worthy candidates and was consistently elevated, respected, and remunerated, teachers would be artists at their craft and rubrics would be unnecessary. Reprising a familiar rant, a content-rich, natural way for children to spend their day, fully engaged in systems, would nullify the need for a scoring tool absolutely obsessed with outcomes rather than process. I am not dreaming. These people who can deliver this are out there, and they all have already left the profession.

Nothing guides a reductionist, closed, dead method like a rubric. Authentic learning be damned.

(The Almighty) Rubric: "In the Box"

How much energy did the creator of this rubric expend rendering this work of art? The time it took to develop could have been used to gather materials for a lab or to transform the classroom into a museum. Instead, brainpower was used to ponder every single possible error a child could conceivably make. I lose faith in civilization on this one, however painfully amusing. Insulting to children's efforts as they move through their challenges, rubrics prevail. There has been serious, contagious rubric-worship going around for years now. Development of the rubric robs students of their teacher's time, but actually *using* the rubric to grade the papers takes the oxygen completely. Consider someone like me with 120 students studying sixteen to thirty little boxes of info to come up with a fair and reasonable grade.

When education isn't about studying meaningful subjects, intellectually bankrupt inventions, such as the almighty rubric, are necessary.

With a rubric mentality, the activity designed by the teacher to meet the needs of a rubric (absurd) is generally a lazy activity lacking authentic meaning. In other words, to be easily measurable, the activity itself suffers. Reductionist activities are activities that slip through the cracks on the high-interest continuum, are not open-ended and thought-provoking, or lead to a new activity in the mind of the learner. Rubrics are tailored to someone else, not you.

If you haven't already, please look at sample rubrics to "enjoy" the ride fully.

Like no other thing, a rubric stands in the way of authentic teacher-student interaction. That's what it's meant to do so there's no argument about grading. This is a pure unadulterated school protection plan. It's come to that, parents can be tough. A rubric is a contract of sorts.

As a teacher, I was a rubric victim as well. In an evaluation, one box included things that did not pertain to my lesson or me. When I asked my supervisor with, I'm sure, a perplexed tone of voice, he said, "That was in the rubric; I didn't make up the rubric."

"So you're going to write things that had nothing to do with my lesson?"

"Yes."

As long as the evaluator likes *most* of what's in the rubric box, the box prevails. On another occasion, I was out for six weeks for surgery and the evaluation read, "Compliance with the expectations of the Uniform Grading Profile is at risk for homework and classwork. The curriculum offers numerous opportunities for classwork and homework to be assigned and graded." What kind of person would write something so demoralizing when a workhorse of a teacher always goes above and beyond and is noncompliant because of absence? It was in the rubric...

Myopically focused, a rubric represents what someone else wants you to know. That's not necessarily a bad thing but when it's rammed down your throat, day in and day out, in every subject, it sends the message that this is insipid, rote, soul-crushing busywork and you are less than a pawn. It becomes a barricade to vivacious learning, rolling out irrelevant, sterile, empty techniques and vacuous benchmarks. As the junk food of education, this mentality gives the false impression of evaluating authentically. There is no denying that you're just in the box.

(The) Running-on-Sentence, SENTENCE

In the Sprout House primary school, a teacher woke up in the morning and looked at "the day" first before moving into what was next on the curriculum. Was there special weather, meteorology, news items, or personal stuff going on in the lives of the class's members? In other words, was there something in the immediate environment that the children should study? This is known as "the emergent curriculum". First things first. After ticking off all those boxes, we would move to the concepts, skills, and enlightenment of the day. Balancing hard work challenges with refreshment and relaxation.

Unfortunately in my school district, the only refreshment is ill-guided candy (chemical candy, not even good candy), distributed by well-meaning teachers. There is no teachable moment, except by a teacher who takes a giant risk of getting caught doing it. So is it any wonder that children's test scores are steadfastly low, year in and year out?

An on-going mystery is that the children of this township cannot stop at the end of a sentence when they read aloud. I have taught fifth grade and middle school here and my experience has shown that children just read and read and read flat words with illogical inflection or no inflection. I am mystified by this phenomenon. Is it the incorrect assumption that fast reading is great reading? Stopping at a period just slows down the show. Is that it? I don't know. I *do* know that this widespread practice should serve as a mirror to the world. We have traded authentic relevance for flimsy tinsel. What have we promoted?

SCHOOL Shouldn't Suck

Where and when did the notion of drudgery become synonymous with school? Mini jokes about school and childbirth are part of the culture and need to be to be whiplashed out of our consciousness. Any misery involved with school is a tragedy. Five glorious hours a day to just LEARN! What I would not give to have that luxury at any age! If done right, it's like college! Or better. Yes, certain frameworks need to be mastered or memorized, but the student, in a productive setting, will *want* to do this. To pick a fruit and savor it and then move on in a purposeful and thoughtful way should be nothing less than an inherent right. Demand contemplation when someone jokes about the drudgery of school.

Season's Greetings

I grew up in a multicultural neighborhood: Irish, Jewish from many places, Scottish, Italian, Sicilian, English extraction, French Canadian, and a few from Scandinavian countries and more, always changing. The moms had card games weekly, at night, in what was apparently warm and positive regard from a kid's standpoint at least. It was the way we were and it was all I knew. However, it was, of course, painful for the Jewish kids at Christmastime to not have Santa.

These types of things are the tiny downside of peace-loving neighborhoods. The Christian kids felt left out when the Jewish kids got to take school days off for their holidays. This is the way it was. N.I.P. Nothing is perfect. Plan ahead. We tried to enjoy each other's holidays. Our teachers helped us do that. We sang each other's songs and ate each other's food. N.I.P., but it worked. And, we learned to say, "Season's Greetings." It was a divine solution! It made it all a sigh smoother than before. I don't know who thought it up, maybe someone at Hallmark got a bonus for it—bravo to them. Now our less-than-perfect solution is under attack by the "Christmas police." What a pity. N.I.P. but please don't assault our successful intercultural experiences. This, I am afraid, is big.

Self-Contained: Ode to the

Nourishment and control are the hallmarks of a teacher who loves the self-contained classroom, with the understanding it will, on average, only last a school year for these specific children. It is an orchestration of timing, depth of subject, project suggestions, enthusiasm, and sometimes strong coaxing. This is not a democracy; it's a benign dictatorship. I want to connect every subject, from social studies to music, foreign languages, and art. I could even do phys. ed. That said, I reserve the right to worship skills just for skills' sake. I know when I want to go lightly and when I want to practice immersion in other areas. Class size must be sixteen or less.

It is automatic that self-contained teachers reflexively are highly accountable to their students and their design. Common Core standards can be used for guidance only. They **will** use it when it's not an edict. Common Core could be a lovely instrument.

The person you marry gets to see you even when the "off button" is pushed. That's the irony of marriage. The same is true of the self-contained class. You're together constantly during everyone's on and off buttons. That's a lot of "off," but miraculously it all works out (at least before Common Core, which was the last time I did it). Not to go Pollyanna, but there is something delightfully euphoric about these self-contained conditions when a *master* teacher is involved. Project ideas flow (see Flow) into the teacher's awareness as he goes about his personal life, because life is and should be about growth and richness. He notices more things because he's unconsciously, constantly scanning for ideas for every individual, and processing current events into pint sizes. Good deeds are free and easy in self-contained classes. Greatness fosters greatness. This is a mitzvah without even feeling the effort. When the teacher feels as if there is no labor in it, it's like the day you realize that you are riding the two-wheeler. The teacher comes to school pumped to engage his class every day, especially on Mondays.

Sell-outs: Education and Otherwise

I was not the girl on the horse, but I *was* at Woodstock. I was mostly a deer caught in the headlights. Remove "mostly." I was completely a deer caught in the headlights. Although there was a lot of nasty, smelly, uncomfortable mud (thankfully not cold), it was just plain awesome to be with so many brave and interesting people, drugs aside. Where are they now? Too many have been wearing suits these intervening decades. Really? Was I so blindsided that I misinterpreted that showmanship for authenticity?

Is human nature so profoundly self-preservationist that consummate selling out becomes a requirement?

Since the '70s, the education community knew what was best for American schools through the enlightened pedagogy of Jonathan Kozel, A.S. Neill, C.A. Bowers, Ivan Illich, Fritjof Capra, Paulo Freire, Ron Miller, William Crain and Jean Piaget, to name only a few.

We knew that bland text, inert activities, disregard for mastery, mediocre literacies, sit-in-the-desk reductionism, and absence of choice, could not arouse many kinds of learners. We keep our absurd school models, like the Vikings attempting a colony in Greenland for 400 years, determined to persevere/suffer. (At least they had the sense to give up the idea of North America with the obvious presence of many societies.)

Absurd school models linger strongly because Pearson pays better with less work.

Sexual Assault

According to the NJ *Star-Ledger*, (2021), four urban teens committed a sexual assault on a female student in the height of nation's blockbuster stories of surprisingly famous or prominent people being punished severely for doing the same. Almost every field of business has rendered a criminal and yet these kids committed the crime and taped it proudly and then they hit "send!"

Two things pop into my mind with crushing obligation. When is "current events" *ever* going to make it into the curriculum? Not only is it mercilessly urgent, but it can drive all the other subjects—the mother of curriculum. Stop searching for stupid examples of context and use real material. Oh but then we might not need Pearson as much, silly me!

The second thought is that no matter how much preaching (paid programs or administrators' threats), kids use this vacuous bravado as their currency. It provides their station in life and that's their value; it's as good as money. Taking them kayaking instead of bringing in paid, onerous programs will render much more meaningful mileage.

Shellshocked

With great respect for those involved in combat areas of the world, I know that I have traumatic stress syndrome from my experiences in a troubled middle school. The violence or fear of violence is present to a minor degree. I am not even close to being consumed by it for some strange reason, but it is a small factor. Rather, it's the administrative, personal, and systemic chaos that bothers me. Coming to school a week early in late August has always been satisfying and contemplative. Making the classroom a lovely place goes a long way. For the past two years, my classroom has had around six holes in the ceiling with water draining down the inside of the walls down to the floor, resulting in topographic buckling enough to trip a person. The first year the floor was fixed in time for me to enter the room with the children, not one minute sooner. No plants, no flowers, no books, no learning centers, and no butterfly rearing. You never quite recover from that, but you do try. Then there's the "m-word," growing slowly... black and powdery, still flourishing above my head, which is now the second year of not getting in ahead of the students, but alas the floor is again fixed by the students' first day, not the ceiling. So we're now in another room, all makeshift and ugly. I can rise to this occasion.

I'm now told I will teach two different grade levels of science. Double work, same pay. Not happy, but still alive. Next news flash, I will travel to another room to teach the other grade level. I will travel back and forth between two floors after every period, alternately with a cart. There's no equipment, no rocks, minerals, weather station, learning centers, library, file cabinet, desk, etc. in the other room. I am sharing this room with another middle school teacher and a third teacher from the night school of students who were asked to leave the daytime high school. At 4:15, I go into that room after setting up my first room, put the Objectives, "Do Now" and Homework on the board for the next day to have the night school erase it all. So much for preparation.

During the 2010–2011 school year, we had twenty-one false fire alarms, which put us on the street sometimes for thirty minutes in January with no coats. No one directed us to a shelter. Teachers all had coats on but not students. I brought my coat and we each wore it for a minute. My students and I practiced hippo or water buffalo protection. We got in a circle with a different person in the middle for a minute each, just as adult hippos would put a vulnerable baby in the middle. We flipped front to back also. I finally found shelter for my class, I had to.

We were told the end of the marking period was Friday. It was also in writing. On Monday of that week, we were told it was moved up to Wednesday. My exam was scheduled for Tuesday and I had 110 students. Each student had three open-ended questions. I couldn't grade it or record it in time.

It goes on and on and on.

SHIFT the Specialist

An urgent shift long overdue is the system of "specialists" in the school building. We have too many administrators, guidance counselors, speech therapists, child-study teams, behavioral specialists, language arts specialists, math specialists, etc. Call me a simpleton, but if you counted up all those people who float around the building, a good portion of the day, and have plenty of time for looking at each other's weekend pictures and used that number of people to become classroom teachers, we'd take class size way down to "fifteen and under" and avoid the problems for which specialists are needed in the first place. Highly technical things like speech therapy could be addressed in a more no-nonsense way. They all lead to the cursed "pull-outs!" Some districts coordinate this carefully—pull out with a language arts specialist *during* language arts. It's not carefully done everywhere; in fact, when it's done haphazardly, it <u>causes</u> kids to become confused and therefore get behind. Far behind.

Simple News Flash (for solving the low-performing urban school dilemma)

If master teachers were to keep their elementary students for two to three years, self-correcting systems would emerge:

1. Short and simple "in-take" test:

   A **choice** of a baseline open-ended type questions would be given on day one in September to demonstrate language arts skills. There would also be a choice of three questions in content area subjects. This would result in a general assessment of skills and knowledge.

2. A simple twenty-question math assessment at the beginning of this teacher-student relationship would contribute crucial starting points. No multiple choice. There would be two or three age-appropriate, open ended questions and a variety of short answer calculations.

3. At the end of each year, the exact same **type** of test would be administered for the **teacher's** own benefit. At the end of the contractual time, the governing body would evaluate the results of those children who attended the longest, etc. Those results would inform **progress, not grade-level equivalence, and be used in a fair way to guide and coach the teacher.**

4. The teacher would have access to all the programs in which urban schools have invested (many) over the previous years, pick and choose the materials that work for their students, individually, collectively or both, use authentic activities and watch the children blossom. Teachers will be totally responsible to balance rigor, comfort levels, stress, and childrens' development of self-motivation. Conversely, teachers who don't have the necessary drive to invest in the process will opt out voluntarily.

Singing

Endorphins are released by the tenth lyric, language comes rolling off the tongue; it's reading.... then effortless memorization. Sorry to be so analytical about singing...Fifth graders, if approached correctly, aren't too cool to sing uncool old-time songs (or science or history songs). In the beginning, they will comply because they view it as "not real work." They won't admit it to each other but they have strong ideas about requests. It's interesting that they don't care if holiday related song is out of season.

Reading? Singing lyrics is powerfully effective pedagogy.

Music time is another reason why a self-contained, cross-curricular classroom is an awesome framework.

Skating through the Woods Near the River

The moments in a life, when you know it's a phenomenon with an amorphous sense of wonder, hopefully occurs for all humans. Shame to waste all the intricacies and capabilities of this ambitious and striving brain of ours.

The woods next to my backyard continue on to be a swamp and finally the Passaic River. When my children were about seven and eleven, I took them and their age-mates (dear friends) from Sprout House one afternoon, in winter, back to my house with everyone's ice skates. I had been watching conditions closely (temperature consistency for days on end, precipitation, and wind). This river has two different county parks on either side, but they are linear parks; they narrowly continue along the river for miles and miles.

The sight of pure "glass" in every direction made everyone decline a snack to lace up those skates promptly. The swamp was transformed into a mythical-quality place where you could make your own course, debate nature with yourself and move on anywhere. Negotiating trees was easy and we also created obstacle trails so we could follow each other because there were, of course, the scratchy blade lines in the ice.

Skating is pretty sublime because, like swimming, humans are having a rush because of the different relationship with the forces such as friction and gravity. Then add going where you want to go, rather than around in circles, and the result is indisputably different. Euphoria? Not even a question.

Does this take planning and hard work contemplating safety on the part of the adult? Planning and work, but it's not hard at all, if you "live" on the planet and dwell effortlessly in the rhythm.

It's been decades since that day, and although we've come close to those perfect conditions, I haven't seen it exactly again.

Sloppy Crap

Patience needed. When I take my grandson to the park, I can't avoid bumping into all sorts of summer camps that might be emptying out of a concentrated activity onto a public playground for some free time. But do counselors (teens almost exclusively) have to put earbuds in and sit on swings so disconnected from any guarantee of safe supervision? Backs to kids on high apparatus, this must double as the counselors' free time too. I am not talking about just one park. I am talking about any park across three counties. Is it the day-camp industry? Apart from the so-called free time, how about the crappy "authentic" activities? Wilderness Camp that advertises making teepees when what they really did was watch an adult assemble a teepee for a solid hour. Fossil activities that consist of burying unrelated fossils in a sand box and showing enthusiasm when a seven-year-old digs it up, libraries offering "Build a Bridge" for six-to-nine-year-olds where the fine motor coordination of that age group defies connecting popsicle sticks with ribbons, hot glue guns in only one hour to do it, including lectures and power point presentations. And the children are not allowed to use the limited glue guns; a counselor must do that part. Shocking schlock... "Tinker Time" is advertised, but supplies are not organized in any way. Dangerous computer parts are mixed in with nuts and bolts. Serious dust from broken down computers is in our lungs and nostrils, as we try to create artistic sculptures from the materials. Food science class is choosing three out of five ingredients to put in the blender that's dirty from being used by the previous kid. Make a bug craft to fill time after a nature walk. Wanton use of feathers, glitter, brand new paper....Church camp with lecturers from a Clean Ocean Group. Kids are just standing around or sitting cross-legged on the floor for way too long. Another camp favorite is Christmas in July. Wait, what? Christmas comes too often as it is. This time it's decorations, music, and no presents. Most residential sleep-away camps are the epitome of authenticity. How did the day camp version get so crappy?

Since these activities aren't really engaging, just add sugar. Treats will always smooth over the frustration of sloppy crap until the sugar rush implodes. But I think they meant well.

So Now I'm Picturing

So now I'm picturing Carly, Annie, De'Nita, Jerome, Octavia, Antoinette, Jessica, Francisco, Ebony, Jeffrey, Terique, Kadir, Kevon and everyone else who has ever brought me a shell or seed pod or fox fire. As they walk home after finding a treasure and then stash it in a sock drawer and protect until the next school morning. This little process is so damn sacred and yet when they present it, knowing the magnitude of the offering, I can't really use enough words to thank them. My face and use of the object will never even top my awe, imagining how it all acted out. *They* might not even "get" how big it is. What *are* children doing when they give you something? My own offspring, nieces, nephews, and grandchildren have the look of genuine bliss upon their presentations in person. When we go on school field trips, my students get this same immediate, hopefully satisfying ecology. Now extrapolate how immense it is when they do it in private, package it up, and deliver it. That is, for *me, picturing it,* a standstill moment, the intersection of warmth and reverence.

So-Called Problem-Solving in Testing

With the advent of standardized testing, we've given false power to the so-called god of "problem solving." It empowers the notion that *the way an adult tester thinks about things is more important than the way the child constructs reality.* (It applies to adult test-takers, of course, too.) A child could know a subject through and through, in and out, high and low, and still not get the nuance that a person from an adult perspective (and possibly different culture) the testing company is looking for. The child's particular "take" is disrespected as "wrong."

Testing companies are also very likely to word questions poorly:

When is the coldest part of the night? A. At sundown B. At midnight C. At 3 a.m. D. At the moment before sunrise. The answer (D) defied the logic of my sixth graders because the word "sunrise" threw them off. They knew all the weather concepts (high pressure, low pressure, humidity, precipitation, water cycle, sublimation, etc.) but people who don't know my students got to decide what would test their "problem-solving" health.

This question was one of only three! This three-question exam was my yearly evaluation as a teacher.

Socrates Worried about the Pen

Socrates thought that the entire civilization would crumble because the invention of the pen would be such a laziness-promoting device that no one would memorize anything anymore. Memorization was, of course, held in high regard and easy writing would be used as a crutch to remember the great things that should just be a part of oneself.

The same fears arose when Gutenberg's printing press made its debut in 1488.

We're now thoroughly launched into a technology that is altering societies, lifestyles, and the way humans think and feel. At the tender age of sixty, I have one foot in the new camp and the other also firmly embedded in the conviction of being thoroughly grounded on a planet with gravity, friction, capillary action, metamorphosis, earthquakes, rising rivers, auroras, and bacteria. Embracing the notion that we are beings in an electro-magnetic field surrounding Earth, digital life seems like a natural and pleasant circumstance. Some of the sillier practices of digital life will hopefully filter out. In school settings there is a great rush to exercise all the postmodern technological inventions as an end in themselves but also as tools to get to something else. My expert opinion is that babies to middle schoolers need huge quantities of the **real** thing before they *represent it* with or without symbols. That said, I believe that each teacher needs to craft a classroom that suits his or her style and students. No administrator should mandate 25 minutes of learning how to use staplers, remote controls, wikis, spray bottles, Power point, zippers, etc. per day. All technology should be at the discretion of the teacher for what that teacher is trying to accomplish.

Let me digress for a moment, to illustrate some more points about technology. Can you imagine a world without socks? In the summer, maybe; in the winter, not so much. I have a little love affair with the cozy feeling of having my ground-hugging appendages in a soft, warm, protected environment. Life, obviously was livable before this technology, but it probably made humans lose a touch of toughness. The "invention" <u>had</u> to be a whole new dynamic of subtle, sublime comfort. Perhaps with so much stress on upright locomotion, humans wouldn't have such good luck with health if there were no socks. We'll never know all the answers to alternative scenarios. What good teachers do know is that young humans need experiences with reality or the building blocks will topple with only symbols for supports. Small doses of memorization propels a desire for more and more internal frameworks. Technology is what makes humans powerful. We don't have good fur, good claws, speedy running ability, killer teeth, or venom. Our modus operandi is a big brain and as the dormouse in Alice in Wonderland famously said, "Feed your head." Good teachers would like the respect for making good judgment calls. If a teacher thinks that a field trip to map the neighborhood storm drains is a better activity than skyping with another class on another continent about the water cycle—that's his class and his decision. The next year, with a different class, he may do the opposite.

Our students excel at technology acquisition. They breathe technology and exhale information. They certainly have instructed me on many occasions. There's no question that their neuron formation reflects these effortless skills. The Socrates in me wants them to also have a poem in their hearts and/or the ability to exponentially pipe it out to the ends of the earth…. maybe.

Something Smells Funny

Something smells funny…. unions? How could a blessed thing like a union turn into a less than good thing? Since my teaching style is consuming of all my personal time, I could never squeeze "union" time into the equation.

The union was always there for me. But math wizards weren't required when previous NJ governors gave away the store in future benefits because decent pay raises were supposedly prohibitive. The union did anything it could to help teachers. Unions, like lawyers, have laser-like singular focus on nothing but the objective. That's their job, but shouldn't it be someone's job to monitor the outcomes for ethical responsibility? I did not protest to those around me that it was a bad move to skip away with a lovely pension at age fifty-five. I wasn't in public education when that manna came from heaven, so I couldn't really protest. It would have been sour grapes as a private school teacher. But it's come back to haunt the folks who didn't do their math homework. It didn't add up then and it obviously doesn't now. It mirrors the Greek people, when the Euro made cash flow like honey only to end up like fly paper.

Now NJ's teacher pensions might evaporate greatly due to expedience. The sweepstakes mentality of the "take what you can, when you can," has backfired. The unions should have taken a position that was "right" in the end, for the end, for *all* taxpayers. Last but not least, the fancy salaries and offices of the full-timer union officers is obscene.

Soul-Searching Moments

We have gotten to the point that everyone in my fifth grade class, can, almost all of the time, identify a correctly constructed sentence. However they don't write many correctly constructed sentences in their journals. I am not just talking about this fifth grade class, but thirty or more years of teaching, urban, suburban, in all socio-economic groups. It always happens. This is a delicate matter. I imagine a demarcation line when the creative baby-brain turns into the logical not-so-baby brain. Edith Cobb talks about it in her book *The Ecology of Imagination*. I imagine that when the transformation happens, all what's known about correct sentence structure will magically transform into perfect writing. The trade-off of baby-genius to serious business is not so bad really. The old creative infrastructure is still there because no adult destroyed it, but a new correct sentence infrastructure is also there. I believe in the power of neuron connections doing amazing things. How intrusive can a teacher be? How intrusive can a great teacher be? Every word of their journals is pure poetry. How do you correct that? There are ways if you take the time to ponder them. A very attentive teacher will keep both possibilities alive and well. Do it the best way you know how. If you are a soul-searching person/teacher, trust yourself.

Sprout House

I couldn't quite send my little girl to pre-school when she was three or four, so how could I send her to kindergarten? Always looking at every leaf, vine, slug, and hermit crab, her quiet intellect was something I just couldn't disturb. Homeschooling wasn't common and I wasn't brave enough to do it. I opened my own small school even with an infant strapped to me. I had so many people helping me do it. It was apparent, they "got" my desperation. We all deferred any kind of remuneration, until sometime "later."

St. Paul's Episcopal Church absolutely cradled us and also deferred rent because the minister, Reverend John and the Vestry channeled a mitzvah in our direction.

The building had a small green yard, an adjacent town playground, and a nice section of woods beyond the playground. The public library was next door and we were in the middle of a cute downtown area. Sounds like a movie set, right?

Wonderful teachers, parents, and children coalesced into a school that honored authentic learning and a content-rich curriculum where we studied more macro-invertebrates by 10 a.m. than most people do all year. It was a place where everyone knew that unless you were on Antarctica, you would *always* be less than ten feet from a spider. It was a place where children could make bread (we called it pretzels) "with their eyes closed." Seriously, without a recipe for sure, because many of them couldn't read yet anyway!

Elementary age kids averaged three plus field trips per month designed and executed by their teacher.

After fifteen years, I decided that I was a failure at achieving diversity, and I was a failure at paying teachers a living wage.

Sprout House succeeded without me, although the elementary grades did not, the preschool, kindergarten, Afterschool Program and Summer Camps are still charming children in nature, to this day.

Standardized tests should be administered the FIRST day of school.

Fraudulence in testing can be opaque, subtle, laughable, or horrifying. Middle school language arts and math teachers receive students from many elementary schools. They may or may not pore over the details. One thing is for sure, they notice the trends. When one elementary school has consistent high scores and drastically low-performing students, everyone rolls their eyes. Here are some stories I've heard. A language arts specialist in a certain elementary school would thump on the desks when she saw wrong answers as she covered for teachers' bathroom breaks during tests. Guidance counselors would call students for make-up tests when the students hadn't been absent. A team of auxiliary personnel would take test booklets and erase "stray marks."

If the tests were given on the first day of school, we would still have some illegal activity, but the authentic retention of material would be clear across the board. Although some parents, of course, would invest in coaching classes in August, the playing field would be slightly more relevant.

Standing Near My Classroom Doorway

Standing near my classroom doorway, on the second floor, of my elementary school, I commissioned an adult to do double-duty as he was seriously working on bulletin boards and decorating the door itself for an entire morning (really only two hours). His secondary mission requested by me, was also serious research. He was to describe and count the way children left the room to go to the bathroom or on an errand. He only did it when there was one individual at a time. By the time the decorations were complete, he hit the thirty mark. Twenty five students did some kind of whimsical walking (skipping, humming, jumping, tapping on lockers, tossing an object, swinging an object). Only five walked normally. Fourteen students were first graders and sixteen were fifth graders.

Reversing the amount of play time vs. symbol-time (letters/numbers), in light of our dreadful test scores, would demonstrate versatile thinking on the part of the adults, based on what they do in an open space like a hallway. Just sayin'.

Suffering

The elephant is truly in the room for some middle school children. Many of the teachers in my school, mutter and come close to weeping over the curious behavior of some of our students. We are slayed by their dismal grades. We watch the suffering manifest in hallway running races, locker slamming, classroom door slamming, poking, slapping, and tripping each other while smiling. "We're just playing." The lunch periods in the cafeteria have a paradoxical look. Screaming, laughing, running, poking, and "snatching" lunches by some, compared to the very serious students hovering over their trays with one arm outstretched as the other hand works the spork. The bizarre feature, is how jolly it all looks with no tinge of anger. It's just dangerously silly in the main. I know. I've been hurt a few times by accident.

When I don't understand something, I hear a hypothetical litany: Incarceration, Jim Crow, Redlining, Discrimination, and Bondage. Incarceration, Jim Crow, Redlining, Discrimination, Bondage, and the resulting frustration. How can people hurt by crippling, vicious institutions come up for air? Some of my students are the offspring. There are many terms for this, one of which is "post-traumatic cultural suffering." Reparations are overdue...Extremely overdue.

Certain negative behaviors become embedded and complicated. The entertainment factor for the children who have not been affected, who consistently show self-discipline, is still very powerful. They know they should appear to be entertained and offer obligatory chuckles, and the cycle continues.

Of all the categories of suffering through school, it's hard to imagine more complexities than those of LGBTQ students. Some if not all Native

American nations held Non-binary people in special regard. When power shifts, perceptions shift. Now is the time to focus on doing the right thing.

Summer Pipe-Dream for My Students

I'd like to run a summer camp for kids who are stuck in cemented cities but don't want to be there July and August.

Kids would attend two-week sessions.

My camp would be located near a large lake. I would have sailing instructors and sailboats. I would have kayak instructors and kayaks. Kids would have one or the other for a three-hour stretch every day with the objective of becoming moderately proficient. Swimming would be part of each session.

Every day would include a thirty-minute small group meeting time with a counselor to discuss the day's current events.

A craft/art session would be once or twice per week according to a sign-up choice. Sometimes the activity would be "advertised" and sometimes not. All activities would be high-quality skills, not catalog-type, stupid, wasteful junk.

A nature hike would be once or twice a week according to sign-up choice. Mapping, compass skills, history, topography, species, rocks, minerals, stream studies, and ecosystems would be a few areas covered. Cooling off in a stream or lake afterward would always be an option.

Pick-up games of volleyball, basketball, and ping-pong would have an official time slot but also occur during free time.

Cooking/Food Science responsibilities would result in the actual meals. For each individual, twice per week.

A high-quality library would be available.

Evenings would include practice on a short skit in small groups to be presented (or not) at the end. (Choice of acting or crew options)

A night hike would occur once a week.

Rotating meal clean-up responsibilities would be required.

These activities all require an expanding acquisition of physics, chemistry, social studies, arts, geology, biology, fitness and health.

Age-eligible, former campers would qualify for future counselors.

Other options, within reason, would always be available for each activity.

Wherever the money comes for the preachy programs could be diverted to good summer camps.

Teach 'Til the Bell Rings (and other confusing procedures)

"Teach 'til the bell rings AND stand in the hallway to monitor discipline" is the school mantra from administrators to teachers. Yes we know there are (deadbeat) teachers who collect papers nine minutes before the bell and let the students slowly pack up, chat, and socialize in or out of their seats. Those same teachers allow socializing for the first five minutes and then five minutes of "settling down." How do I know this? Because that is the expectation of kids when they first become my students. They are flabbergasted that they get "reminded" if the "DO NOW" work isn't completed and homework isn't submitted immediately.

So now EVERYONE is told "teach 'til the bell." What does this mean? "Papers" need to be collected, homework explained, etc. At least two students have a private question for teachers afterwards. Previously absent students need to schedule make-up work. Teachers are penalized for not standing IN the hallway while classes change.

All logic is tragically lost when all teachers are treated the same, and yet, how can you not?

Teachers are supposed to be available to kids for help at the end of the day. But in my middle school, we must walk students down three flights to the outside door, then bring them back up for help (or heaven forbid, detention). They don't stay on their own anymore, because the dismissal procedures are so confusing. If detention is necessary, I can no longer say "stay" with the option of coming tomorrow with a note to a parent explaining why. Now I must call home to get permission for detention. Where is my phone budget and when do I do any of this if I "teach" 'til the bell?

Amidst all of the disorder, where is that comfortable place a student can hang out for a few minutes at the end of the day?

Teacher of the year/Attacked the next year/ Dialect and Ambiguity

When I first transferred to the school where I taught fifth grade, the principal liked the fact that I met all my deadlines, never sat down, got good scores on my class's practice tests, had great student enthusiasm, good student behavior, and a beautiful classroom. The previous term, the science supervisor had enthusiastically sold me to the principal. The science supervisor was leaving for some reason and therefore didn't mind that I was leaving the middle school science team for a self-contained fifth grade. Because he made me "teacher of the year," at the end of the year, reveals that the principal agreed with the supervisor.

I was, of course, teaching every subject. Fast forward to Year Two. I tailored the language arts to my students, using grammar examples from our experiences and our names. They ate that up.

It bothered me that I was expected to correct their very lovely, pristine, uniform, spoken, urban dialect. As a person who has studied and appreciated Black Dialect/Ebonics/Street/Code switching since the '70s and now considered Christopher Emdin's work a reference material, I became cranky hearing the harsh corrections of spoken language in the school building. When I innocently asked the building Language Arts Literacy (LAL) specialist if we could have a "script" from the superintendent on her thoughts about how to delicately correct children's *written* work (no way was I going to touch spoken dialogue), a day later, I was the object of the principal's very raised voice in his office.

The downhill plummet began.

Teacher-Led Field Trips

Thank the spirits for environmental educators! We wish they would just take over all the classrooms. Because, if you have a teacher that can run her own nature trip, you have hit the lottery. That person knows all the background for *those specific* children. That person knows their capabilities thoroughly. That person knows the necessary **half-steps** toward the contingent concept. That person is not going to lecture for even a minute on the wrong fact. It will be full-speed ahead euphoria. There won't be squirming. Train the teachers.

Teacher's Day

Think of all the awesome and stimulating things a person can do *for fun* and realize that self-contained classroom teachers (and homeschooling parents) can and should be doing all or some of them almost all the time: observing insects and spiders, swimming, sledding, biking, hiking, fishing, tallying types of trucks that pass, cooking, cleaning, reading, writing, building, crafting, singing, playing instruments, playing sports, dramatizing, kite-flying, telescoping, microscoping, mammal-watching, bird-watching, and *much* more. Teachers get to do this with eager companions. Please don't gripe that your students tune out. They tune out because they've habituated to more sedentary pastimes. This is my unscientific, non-empirical, *firm* conclusion. *I'm right.* It's a 100 percent correct conclusion. No elementary-age kid at Sprout House ever tuned out of this kind of learning.

Pinch me, because I would look around and whisper in my head, *How great is my day?*

Teachers/Administrators

Although a teacher can transform their teaching skills on a self-improvement plan, early on in a teaching career, individuals notice that they need to get a master's degree to climb the salary scale effectively. A master's is thirty-three credits. Two master's degrees (or a PhD) are even better. It's work to be sure. It's also expensive. Folks who are not committed to being in the classroom can simply get an administrator's certificate for eighteen credits and make boatloads of money instantly if they get the job. Follow the logic. Committed people stay in the classroom, take lots of graduate-level courses, give up weekends to write papers, etc. and make less money than the individuals who take eighteen credits that do not include nearly as much on curriculum, development and psychology. The latter group now is in charge of the fate of the former group.

The Collapse of Thrift

On a micro level, some of the following scenarios demonstrate education practices that are arrogant with taxpayer money and disregard for the planet. Some show the opposite. It might not have anything to do with taxpayer consideration, just a genuine teacher who automatically avoids wastefulness and respects the planet.

A parent was asked if she would take home a bunch of staplers that were jammed and try to free them since I didn't see any bent parts. After months of constructing 3-D math projects, the staplers were tired. The lucky parent was stunned, "Throw them out ….you have a budget."

Rip down the background paper on the bulletin board (miles and miles of it) and crumple it in the trash. Tear up brand-new paper for collages.

The students are leaning on the balance scales for fun and the pans and other parts are getting bent. It's unpopular to redirect them constantly. New scales need to be purchased.

It is much easier to order the tadpole kit (entire) than gathering pond water every other night for classroom tadpoles that have been temporarily borrowed from the pond. Another option is to just go study the pond and take nothing.

Taking ten one-ounce sand samples from various NJ shore towns for a comparison learning center, results in a rainbow of mineral colors. Also taking ten one-ounce soil samples from various physiologic regions of NJ., does the same. This is part of the definition of sand and soil. Order it from a science materials company instead.

We don't use **that** kind of lined paper anymore. "Chuck it."

Too fussy for homemade planters. Throw some kid-mixed composted soil into a bucket with drainage holes drilled by a parent and voila. Or better yet, re-use old ones. Generate more plastic usage by buying new.

Look at the garbage that goes out. Much of it could be collage and 3-D constructs in art class. The biggest expense in a garden program is the soil. Make it with a composter from school lunch waste. Pay attention to care-less use of expensive equipment. Look around for any learning opportunity in the environment. In the boom days, I was given $300 classroom budget plus our department was given $1200 per year for a piece of new equipment. Now we get nothing and habits don't necessarily change. Instead the whining increases.

Thinking that anyone should be able to retire at age fifty five, is on the backs of your neighbors, and is the biggest disrespect of economy. This is tax-payer money. Be fair. Play nice.

The Context

School life and life in general, let alone history class, has an all-imposing backdrop, and that is the faceless scourge of slavery. No action and no possession is free of its grip. Visit any historic mansion or research any comfortable scientist or inventor and know that slavery probably played a role in that comfort. If you want to argue the point, delete the word slavery and rest assured that someone was exploited so someone else could be very comfortable. The US economy was built through the construct of slavery. Money doesn't come from a waterfall and history classes need to tell every last detail. Question every awesome thing you see and you might not want to ooh and ah so much when you visit opulence from the past. Taking children to visit historic opulence is a more intense narrative than its fluffy presentation.

The Contradiction of the Hands-On Curriculum

In a middle school setting, the announcement of a hands-on activity renders the audience "excited." The people who are awake are really awake. The hands-on activity commences, and sometimes someone can't contain the excitement. Things get silly and it gets slowly contagious. Most days, things stay on track. On a bad day, lab materials appear on the floor on the other side of the room. Thankfully, the good days far outnumber the bad. The creativity with materials is formidable. Someone is always thinking of another exceptional idea for an experiment. However, the noise level can reach a semi-roar and equipment is not quite in the same condition as the period before. Despite the confusion, faces are beaming, good questions are asked, and concepts can be discussed and applied. Why is there sometimes such a betrayal in the form of low-level chaos? That, of course being a rhetorical question, is one of the essential questions of the middle school modus operandi. Holding the knowledge gained in that hands-on lesson is another story. In stressed schools, students retain it for the duration of the "chapter" **if** the teacher keeps the ball in the air. The top-level students will own the concepts, but for the average student, it could be gone by the midterm, hopefully not.

When all is said and done, I am still convinced that when you breathe life into a lesson, it is by far a more genuine, healthful way to spend the day. By almost all respected accounts, others agree. I believe the benefits of an authentic curriculum are incremental. The more it's done, the "branchier" the brain cells. However, "the state" micromanages urban districts preventing myriad hands-on activities; not because they are hands-on, merely because it's not their script.

Seeing classes just filling in the blanks, period after period is sickening. There are solutions.

The Dead Curriculum

Is there anything alive inside a textbook? It's full of charts and data from somewhere else, probably not your neighborhood. It's full of sentences that you rarely say; yet you are required to underline the verbs. The civics text is full of concepts that are not in the newspaper today. The math text has you calculating rainfall averages for an imaginary place when you could be doing the real ones for your neighborhood. The science text has you predicting the phase of the moon three days from the one pictured instead of the one today.

When a teacher uses local, relevant data, what's the added bonus? You become knowledgeable about your region. What does it require? The newspaper or the internet would be good. Real teachers.

Once teachers start, they can't go back.

The Galaxy in My Coffee

Do you spend time developing observation skills? Do you lead kids to really observe? Without making it a chore, our observation skills hopefully can "rub off" on the small people in our lives. I disappoint myself when I fail to notice things or remember things that I look at constantly. Don't be too hard on yourself because, let's face it, we can get very busy. Just be conscious of the details in your field of vision and share those details. My nephews and grandsons gather around when I stir a cup of coffee because if you trickle in the milk near the perimeter, right after stirring, a spiral galaxy will appear for a few seconds.

Just be conscious.

The Jargon and the Choice

EXAMPLES OF JARGON

Anticipatory set
Rubrics
Item analysis
Differentiated instruction
Formative assessment
Summative assessment
Interactive whiteboards

Data driven

"Partnership" for the Assessment of Readiness for College and Careers (PARCC)

Rigor

"I can" statements

Align the curriculum

Exit ticket

Blended learning

Balanced literacy

College and career ready

Benchmarks

Flip the classroom

Unpack the standards

A bingo game was created with these gems. Instead of yelling "bingo," teachers are advised to yell, "bu** **it."

It's not the effort behind the recommendations that riles teachers; it's the **never-ending** steamrolling of old and recombined dogma that steals valuable professional development time. Good teachers have their own ideas for workshops they would love to attend instead.

The Lay of the Land

The learning issues of certain school systems are defyingly complex. There's eagerness but there are difficulties with retention—retention meaning "memory retention." There are attendance and punctuality issues. It's hard to master things when you come to school four days a week. There's major pain in putting a grammatically correct, standard English sentence on the line. On standardized tests, in measuring comprehension, there is not always much to relate to in terms of content or vocabulary. Listening to fifth graders read aloud, you realize that almost no one stops at the end of a sentence. Administrators ignore the fact that a precise but different dialect predominates.

Many children are transferred from one school to another often for various reasons. I sometimes only have a few of the same students in June that

I had in September. I've noticed an interesting phenomenon. New students have an amazing capacity for figuring out the lay of the land in one swallow. The names of the administrators, the locations of all school offices, all the stairways, the schedule, the bathrooms, the cool teachers, the uncool teachers, cafeteria rules, how the school works and all the names in the class. That's lots to process and it's done flawlessly. A lot of skills have to intersect to accomplish that much learning.

The Path Has a New Puzzle

The path has a new puzzle around every corner if not every two steps. My friend and I meet every two weeks exactly to study a wildflower trail in a county park. We have done this from early February, and now it is the middle of October. We have watched form and function from sprouts and blossoms, to dried up, crispy stems, leaves, and seeds. Catching these plants in their prime is for amateurs; we boast about much more challenging stages. If you think every berry has a lifespan, you'll be the wiser when you can gauge the life of a fern by the look and position of its spores (such a show-off). Different parts of the trail are micro-habitats for specific species. There are uphill "neighborhoods" and downhill ones. Dry zones and stream partners. The proximity of the various bedrock types and glacial erratics offer the chemistry for soil nutrients for each little wonderland. You can't see it but there's a microbiome too.

We go home and match our photos with the field guides and web sites, argue a little, think a little, sleep on it, and realize some tiny joy. In the interim, everywhere we go, we make connections to cultivated cousins and beautiful weeds.

This is the perfect school. We designed it. We assigned the homework. We know when we need more info and we know when our brains are overloaded, to scale back. We are giddy with our discoveries and most importantly…. super-motivated to do more.

The Right Person For This Profession

It's an extremely subtle requirement: we use the word "creative" so haphazardly. This time what is required is someone who can be creative for 15+ human beings every day and contemplate them every night. No small order. Do doctors ponder treatments for their patients, sketch out individual plans, and scour libraries on their vacations, and rummage sales on Saturdays? Someone who stops dead in their tracks, to collect acorns enough for everyone to plant.

The "someone" has a high level of sophistication, is personally "turned on to his/her own hobbies," who "gets" this kind of academic rigor, even if it is just advanced "kite flying" or advanced beachcombing, or loves to play rock music in a band. As Joseph Campbell coined the phrase, someone who knows how to "follow their bliss." Someone who has a subscription to a specialty magazine. That's the first part.

The second part is not politically correct but it is going to be uttered here: unless you're in Finland, this person is typically not magna cum laude. If they were, they probably would be an astrobiologist or a physicist. This person is a human sponge who likes everything, can think metaphorically, and break things down into smaller and smaller units—a transcendental generalist.

The Spy in the Elementary School

After four years of seeing only my slice of what is surely a very big problem, I became driven to see my students' experience before middle school. I asked for a transfer to fifth grade because the academic problems in middle school were haunting. I felt compelled to seek out the background. I fully expected that when I got there, I might like it and stay there. This was fall, 2006.

My fifth grade class was ironically positioned next to a string of first grade classes with another fifth grade across the hall. It was a cozy old building with beautiful but "distressed" wood wainscoting and trim. There were lovely Sycamore trees shading our windows and cool breezes through large second-floor windows. The building got criticism for being old but I really liked it.

I relished the idea of teaching all the subjects, despite the fact that each subject brought with it lengthy lesson plans. Other teachers were fleeing elementary school for this reason.

The pressure on my fifth graders was palpable. Every day they were required to write ten sentences in their language arts journals. I had one student who could write good sentences, spell well, and form paragraphs. He told me he had nothing he wanted to write about. Most days I could coax our classroom activities out of him. Other days, he just put his head down. My other students tried hard, thought of great ideas, but their work was hardly legible/intelligible. At all costs, my only goal was to maintain an upbeat atmosphere. My second year was a repeat of the first, but my new "writer" loved it and did well. He moved out of the district before Thanksgiving! The language arts "grammar" workbooks were puzzling to me. Most of my fifth graders could identify a noun. Verbs were hit and miss, but I was required to go through the book doing a concept a day: adverbs, adjectives, predicate adjectives. The rest of the fifth grade classes were on predicate adjectives. None of them retained the material. I was still working on nouns and verbs at my great peril and trying to make it relevant using our experiences as the sentences.

One day, a few days into the fall term, the door swung open on a Wednesday afternoon. It was 1:45. We were in the middle of analyzing the weather/climate page in the *Star-Ledger*. We made graphs of precipitation, compared the amounts to previous years, discussed temperature and humidity, and compared our results on our homemade weather instruments. To say we were highly engaged is an understatement. After that, we were about to check homework and move on to the new lesson. Through the door , unannounced, came the building "math specialist."

"Hi boys and girls, I'm going to teach your math lesson today."

I looked at her and said, "We're in the middle of it."

"Not today," she said. "Every Wednesday, I will be here for your math period."

I told the students to put their things away and gave them blank paper. She proceeded to teach them perimeter of a rectangle with no visuals, except for her drawings on the chalkboard. After less than five minutes, she moved on to area of a rectangle. After a few minutes of that, she expected them to absorb circumference of a circle. With plenty of time left to gather books and coats to depart for home, she blazed through area of a circle and volume of a rectangular prism. My students were obediently scratching pencils on paper with a few watery eyes.

To my horror, one day, I heard noise in the first grade next door. Someone was screaming. I ran over. The teacher, my colleague, motioned to me that the student was ok. Later, the teacher told me that the student was stress-screaming because the first graders also were required to write ten sentences a day in their journals. Most of them could only write individual letters.

The language arts specialist in the building (yes, these are your taxes) would constantly, rudely correct grammar in children's conversations with her. This could take place anywhere in front of others. I asked her if we could have a statement from the superintendent on how to handle "dialect." I was called into the principal's office the next day. He raised his voice at me in a very unpleasant way.

Before Thanksgiving, I was un/empirically, emphatically sure that most learning issues in my urban elementary school were adult-induced.

The Strange Reality of Being Face Blind

In the November 2006 issue of WIRED reports on a condition in which patients can not recognize faces, including the one in the mirror. They use clothing and voice cues to identify people. This condition provides strong support for a separate part of the brain devoted to processing faces. "Facial recognition is a hard-wired aptitude that does not depend on learning."

Does not depend on learning....does not depend on learning....How many other quirky, unexplainable conditions must teachers be aware of? All of them. Count on it. Count on a kaleidoscope of differences. Respect them and work toward their best environment. Only then will you be a master teacher.

The Subtleties of Students

When I had small classes of usually eight to ten students at suburban Sprout House, the day was pleasant and the natural humor and cleverness of kids could be appreciated in a contingent way. There was a relaxed amount of time to enjoy each other's rich slice of life.

Imagine having 110 or 120 students. On the bad days, it's nothing less than heart-health threatening. On medium to great days, it's effortless entertainment and lots of warmth and love, despite its natural, breezy, formidable energy. Oodles of kids interacting with each other, striving for novelty. One act plays , with the most clever lines, can be lifted right out of the air all day long. These young brains live in a complex environment, so they are always looking for unexpected narratives. Absorbing dialogue, effortless humor, and flowing creativity are always evident. Occasionally there are negative episodes, but most often it's effortless humor. This drama is consistently underestimated but manifests in intense talent and fascinating ways to look at the world.

The Tyranny of Outcomes

OMG if I hear another word about predictable, measurable, decisively positive outcomes, I will *&%#* The extreme disrespect for allowing a child the luxury of dabbling in a pool of intellectual ideas is completely ignored or prohibited. It is with great risk that I indulge in this activity. The payoff is so profound and my principals/principles for the most part have encouraged and partaken in the enjoyment. There are other levels of inspection that would not savor or appreciate the richness of meandering through a habitat, perusing a science book shelf, identifying the physics as you ride your bike, or a birdwatching experience. The beauty of *finding* the *science in the experience* cannot be accommodated because **it is not measurable!**

Let's just say I knew "this teacher" that had a one-room schoolhouse and found some very tall evergreen trees on the school property. She contemplated safety issues and then allowed third graders to climb to a level they were comfortable with. The first day they only climbed about ten feet, testing the position and location of each branch before moving their feet. Then the next test was the strength of the branch. Calculating the hand positions was simultaneous with the same considerations. The children's focus was intense and silent. I, I mean she, nervously watched in silence. They were evaluating materials and forces bit by bit. The second day, they all (even the timid) went a few branches higher. This time they all seemed to stop and really look around before descending. When one explained what she saw, the others gave descriptions too. By the third day, many people would think the children were just too high up, but it was clear that the same careful considerations from the first day were being employed continuously. They could be heard talking to each other at the top but exactly what was being said was not audible. No one told them not to go too high because they stopped right where the thickness and strength of the tree trunk diminished. They stayed a few minutes longer each day. When they came back down, they related information about the needles, nests, insects, spiders, patterns in branching, and human activity they could view. There was definitely a mild but certain satisfaction if not euphoria. Reading and math went down like honey after the sublime climb.

"Outcomes" are a disrespect for a stunning migration of monarch butterflies through the schoolyard, a sudden recall election in local politics, the latest fabulous wildflowers growing in a vacant lot, a report that the local stream has been degraded, a recent series of rainfall events have precluded drought restrictions and other teachable moments. All these and more are meaningful issues that can be studied by anyone from eight years old and up in an age-appropriate way. Since the power-people didn't put it in "the script," a teacher faces charges for diverting the curriculum if his class is found graphing the year's local precipitation, or researching what is upstream in the contaminated the river. Worse, he might want to go outside and have his students observe the plants on which the monarchs are laying eggs. Oh, back to the script to study the curriculum developed with another state's children in mind. If caught, a note or two in the teacher's file or a stressful rush-job to try to do both. The stress ends up on the psyches of the teacher <u>and</u> the children.

The *notion* of OBJECTIVES itself contradicts self-motivated learning. If infected by a teacher's enthusiasm for something, students become self-motivated. Obviously we need objectives, but zealot-like policing of meaningful divergence leads me to think someone's textbook company-brother-in-law is calling the shots. Wildly imaginative, but what other explanation is there? When things stop being plausible, good teachers are demoralized, not burned out.

Training in the "Emergent Curriculum" held so much promise, was the underpinning for developing great teachers and captured student intellect in such a compelling way that nothing less than a solemn requiem is in order.

The Wisdom in the Muscles

I didn't do it that many times because I was already fourteen when we moved to that house, but I, at least, got to do it. Someone in the neighborhood erected two rope swings from trees on high ridges. One of them just swung gracefully (terrifyingly to some) into the woods. The other swung over a lake created by a gravel company. The latter, we obviously used to jump in the water. What is the payoff? Sensual thrills, an illusion of flight, freedom, a sense of accomplishment and a better understanding of physics for sure. Everyone was always giddy afterwards and no one, as far as I know, got hurt.

My sister reminded me of it recently and I realized it doesn't get any better than that. Having that in my life probably spoiled me but kept me from needing artificial highs. And yet, with the busyness of life, I hardly remembered it until reminded. Events like that are always there, remembered or not. The sensorimotor (Piaget) memory shapes us. I was so lucky to be a child with frequent beach trips, fun in the snow, jumping in the leaves and sticky, staining berry picking.

When kids had a difficult time learning to read (in the '70s), we told their parents to go home and learn to ride a two-wheeler bicycle. That's it.

The wisdom in the muscles, the giggles in the heart, and the salubriousness of nature-immersion was, and is, the aim of Sprout House.

Their Tinkering

The tinkering that passes for education reform is preposterous. More paperwork, different paperwork, less paperwork, mostly MORE. Charts, diagrams, rubrics, data. These are things that kids don't care about. Common planning periods are bullied, demeaning, and dehumanizing. Instead of planning together, you and your partners must complete this form and that form so you never get to the living, breathing part of sharing.

Yes, there are some inept teachers, but this is not about how to help them or weed them out. This is just about how great teachers give up.

There's No Such Thing As a Seagull

The City and Country School in N.Y.C. has a motto: "Learning from Kids Since 1914." Good teachers know that the melding of a group creates new facets of skills and systems, because the brains in a class really become a system after a couple of weeks. By virtue of their virtue, good teachers make this happen without even knowing it. Let the exponential learning begin.

Every individual brings their own stories, knowledge, and skill sets. I have a fondness and deep respect for gulls, so I have always led many estuary and seashore field trips. Deciphering the differences in gulls is a wonderful skill of differentiation, classification, and discrimination. Pink legs, yellow legs, habits, and habitats are effortlessly learned. Sophisticated discrimination like this is a prerequisite for putting together straight lines and curved lines in an alphabet for some children.

After some lofty dialogue about shorebirds, Matthew J. said to me, "You know there's no such thing as a seagull? Look in the field guide." Of course he was right. There are only Black-Backs, Herring, Ring-Billed, Laughing, Bonaparte's, etc., but not one seagull. Clever little brainiac. I love my gulls too.

They Meant Well

In the name of hands-on, meaningful, authentic learning, "we" have produced learning kits, programs, textbook extensions, etc., which are actually far more tedious than not doing it at all. Take for example, a California based program designed collaboratively by teachers and museum educators. I actually liked this program a great deal, but I watched in dismay as other teachers followed to the letter every single module until the kids hated the subject, which was planetary science. My students enjoyed the math calculations to ascertain the size of a certain crater and find it on the map. After two in one week, they were done. I watched another teacher force thirteen calculations. My students enjoyed doing one more a week later. All this was part of a unit that defined five types of craters, simulated craters, and measured depth and width, defined "above" the surface, "even" with the surface, "below" the surface, logged phases of the moon on an ongoing basis, memorized Apollo landing sites, identified eight different moon rock types, analyzed whether they were Maria or Highlands, experimented to determine density of all eight rocks, to just name a few. God bless the developers of these programs, but not all groups of children can hang on that long. I could see that this is the kind of stuff that kids won't complain about because in their hearts they know it's good stuff, but they silently tune out in a big way when the paperwork gets endless and it gets overwhelming. It also flies in the face of individualizing. Teachers need to take responsibility for how students will get to the finish line (state test) and make decisions for *their students* and their program, and design a plan to accomplish those goals. If a certain group of kids are into it, take the ball and run, but knowing the chances are slim, pay attention to the yawns.

This program would make a highly productive afterschool club for interested kids.

This is Not a Democracy

I spend the summer quietly contemplating the following September: the room design, the procedures, the rules, and the activities. It's my new world. When I meet my new students (and they are new to the school in the sixth grade), I show them the luxuriousness of the tiny academic community within our four walls.

The Rules:

1. Respect all people, living things, and classroom objects.

2. Be cooperative, hardworking, and HELPFUL TO SUBSTITUTE teachers.

3. Use good decision-making: no one is ever going to think of every rule to tell you, but you will be held responsible and have consequences if you don't make good decisions.

I give no second chances. (It's just a license to do something negative twice.)

I'm very fair; I set up great activities; I expect good behavior. My consequences are swift and genuine. I'm the ump. When there is occasional, grumpy complaining, my answer is always: "This is a benevolent dictatorship, not a democracy."

I'm the grown-up (with experience who has made a decision to teach them and guide them); they are the children maximizing their experience. That said, there are many alternative, independent schools around the world that give their students the power to hire and fire teachers and judge the behavior of their peers. This is in no way a criticism of them and how they function.

Those Are Not Big Stars

I wake early in winter so I always check on the "night" sky. How else will I be able to tell my students what's happening in the cosmos? The evening sky, from the night before, is only the beginning.

I remind my students to be in the universe, whispered in all the books by Brian Swimme. We forget that we are.

Teachers go over how to tell a planet from a star with your naked eye.:

— "comes out" early in the evening

— changes position every night (against the constellations)

— appears larger than constellation stars

The world of darkness is almost entirely forgotten in today's data-based curriculum. We morph into a somewhat different planet at night. Different active animals, different plant behavior, different weather, different atmospheric patterns. We encounter more **awareness** of being in the universe. Half of our existence is in the dark. Those are not big stars, they are close planets. Everyone should know that. This is one of the true "basics."

I even saw one easily during the two-minute darkness of the totality of the solar eclipse . . in 2017!

Transitional Kindergarten (TK)

When kids miss the kindergarten cut-off date or appear immature to someone/everyone, parents look for a transitional program. I don't know the exact numbers, but parents have been seriously enrolling their kids in them for twenty five years or more. Now California has a publicly funded TK.

Sprout House has always had one. I have a few concerns about large-scale programs. The programs are described as "reading, writing, math, science, art, music....but play-based." So far so good. It goes on to say that these skills are "sneaked into" play or nature walks. Also very good. What bothers me is the notion of running in place, and waiting for maturity. School shouldn't be a wedge in a timeline. It should be perceived as something or the other. That's a little petty, so I will illustrate. If our system is good, why do we need this little crutch? Shouldn't the system be set up to be fine for all kids? "What have we done wrong with kindergarten" is the red flag I see. Worse, I have interacted with many parents who just want their kid to have an advantage (over others). Yikes! On the other end of the rainbow, can you picture almost nineteen-year-olds trapped in high school?

Try This

"Try this…."

"No, this…."

"Try that!"

Nothing is ever given a chance before the next program is rolled out. This is the economy of the greater education industries.

The Tug of Love

The power of the love for a first child is like a train engine. It comes from somewhere and makes you believe in black holes because that "somewhere" is a mystery. Even when they never stop crying, you develop a state of ultra-patience. The adult with a new offspring is now an extraordinarily different person. The gushing enjoyment, concern, and appreciation of this little person supersedes all previous entertainment, attachments, and preoccupations. The love for a baby inspires the epiphany: "Wow, my own parents, loved the 'me-baby' this much too," and is a crazy revelation.

In a quiet, dreamy, fluid way, I was smitten. The euphoria continues through all the young years of discovery. I think that's a record for euphoria. She was a tough, colicky baby and a funny, contemplative, well-behaved little kid. She could hear grass growing. I loved my life.

Miscarriage. Such pain. My friends and relatives were having their second babies and I was having a dilation and curettage. My sweet little child got me through. It helps to have an understatedly, relentlessly wonderful husband.

A year later the little sister came to us like a Christmas morning. We shared in her preciousness, with different awesome emotions. There was now a mirror to view the miracle. I worried a little about the sharing part. Life is dynamic but we're cursed with being conscious. The new circle works miraculously and becomes a celebration and it is fluidly easy.

When teachers witness overbearing parents, they must take into account the essential truths of parenthood. But parents must learn to act in their children's genuine best interest. The teacher wants what's best for the kid in the long run. The parent wants a reptilian, leathery egg shell around the kid…. two kinds of love. There isn't a happy medium; but there's a medium.

Twisted Behavior

What a difference a year makes! School year 2013–14, when new Common Core Curricula Corporations rolled out the goodies, it became the year of Extra Intense Twisted Behavior in middle schools. Teen behavior is always complicated, but when there is a quiz or test literally every other day, humanity starts to unravel. I plan to spend Martin Luther King Day thinking about Martin, sleeping and crying. It's cheaper than therapy.

Urban : Are There Scoundrels Here?

A master teacher, one who raises butterflies in the classroom, has ongoing experiments, prompts children to be researchers, bakes bread to teach physical and chemical changes, sings history tunes, and has students begging to suggest a certain piece of literature, is told to stop what he's doing and follow the "corporate company" Smartboard binder for 180 days. In addition, tedious lesson plans take up all day Saturday and part of Sunday. When he sneaks more meaningful and enjoyable work into the day, it's noted in his file, because the evaluator, who has far fewer years' experience than he does, doesn't endorse it.

The administrator has so many "underperforming" teachers that she is overwhelmed and therefore buys into the corporate program and makes it a mandate for *everyone.* The "underperforming" teachers are either a mismatch to the profession, have been beaten down by dysfunctional procedures to the point of complete weariness, or just can't take the workload. They also have the strong disapproval of district supervisors because only 30 percent of the school passed the language arts and math state tests.

The district supervisor (superintendent's office) is on notice from the state that they must **show** they are doing something about it. So everybody does something. That's why failing schools keep failing. The private companies have a flourishing industry. Everyone at the top is protected for a very long period.

The creative master teacher has a choice—defy, and lose the job in about eighteen to twenty-four months, or comply.

Can a person be vilified for saving their job? The jury is taking too long to decide.

Urban: The Never-ending Gimmicks

Just because we're not saying anything doesn't mean we haven't noticed that what we were chastised for doing last year is now an official program. Roll out PSI, Progressive Science Initiative. It's not even a catchy, clever name. Last year we were to engage our students in never ending hands-on science in the form of labs and learning centers. This year we are to prop them up in front of a smartboard, in groups of three to four and roll out a PowerPoint, embedded short videos, "interactives," and multiple choice questions. The multiple choice questions sink to the bottom of the worst workbooks or work sheets. No day escapes snooze-fest time. Same old problem, putting LOTS of wrong answers in front of students' faces with the multiple choice mentality. Here's how the PSI works. The PowerPoint god is worshipped throughout the period. Each student has hard copy three slides to a page. The group spends part of their time paraphrasing the content of each PowerPoint slide on the hard copy. They help each other to get it right. Fair enough….BUT NOT FOR 180 days!

* From September until midwinter, my class endured this with no Smartboard, just one inch square, poorly photocopied, muddy images! My polite complaints were ignored until something much worse came up. Then I was given the same handouts, but with clearer images.

Urban Realities: Not the Weight-Watchers' Pledge

(2007) Keondre refuses to recite the anti-violence, gang, and drug pledge. He does, however, stand up, when twenty-five other fifth graders recite it with the same nonchalance of dieters saying the weight-watcher pledge.

In my school district, George Bush is blamed for taking away almost all my fifth grade students' science classes. We have to double up on language arts and math. The mayor of our town has taken away all our social studies and art classes for a period of time. We are required to teach an anti-gang initiative program five periods a week. This program is a "kid-friendly" group therapy session. Although it's hardly of any interest. "What's your favorite movie? What did you like about it? What did you dislike? Who is the most supportive person to you? How is that person supportive? Whom are you supportive of? What do you like about your neighborhood? What do you dislike about your neighborhood?" My students see right through these questions and challenge this middle-aged, white lady teacher. Tyronn tells me, "There's nothin' to dislike in my neighborhood! It's fine!" Quickly latching on to the notion that this "session" takes away school time, they remind me about it when I conveniently forget to include it. The good part is that I realized what we can do with all the wonderful energy that we dredge up sitting on chairs in a tight little circle. I co-opted the session for current events discussions…. my kind of current events: the Hubbell telescope, Kofi Annen, Nobel Peace Prizes, the space station, Senator Barack Obama, a new dinosaur fossil, and a Komodo dragon born without an egg.

Process the visit from the police department and Prosecutor's Office …It's an assembly for second to fifth grade. The kids are all chanting the answers to these questions: "Should you ever touch guns? Should you ever do errands for your neighbors if your mom doesn't know? Should you try drugs?"

Why not let us enrich our students' lives instead of scaring them? Can't school be magical and engrossing? Won't that ward off gang membership as well as anything? Take the thousands and thousands of dollars spent on the implementation of these programs and send the fifth graders to their choice of sailing camp, surfing camp, sleep-away camp. "Programs" in urban schools are now a lucrative industry and the stakeholders aren't going to give it up easily.

We're beating a dead rat if we persist with all the preachy convictions (2004–2007).

Under the same edicts of the first year teacher, master teachers (creative, hardworking, results-getting, student-motivating) are ridiculously lowered to humiliating levels. Subject to things like "rewrite your behavioral objectives on the board so students can see the three parts," instead of "thanks for setting up that exhilarating chem lab six times yesterday and cleaning it up till 6 p.m.," we endure. You know, the lab that will improve their math and language skills because *they wrote it up correctly and asked for something else like it* ,or *thanks for taking 120 students over three days to a local hiking trail to analyze outcroppings of bedrock, catalog plants, and animals and follow a topographical map, AND thank you for finding six retired science teachers to volunteer with the groups*. So instead of putting their energies into things that matter, to help students, master teachers are hunched over their laptops all day Sunday tinkering with behavioral objectives. There just isn't any more time to give when you mark papers every night till the clock hits midnight (middle school teachers have over a hundred students). We gain one step for clear objectives and fall back three steps for not giving kids the educational equivalent of rapture. The most challenged first year teacher is told to "stay on the same page as the grade level subject colleague." This will never promote mastery and confidence. This is sad enough, but unconscionable to disrespect the designs of the great veterans and creative novices.

Teachers are required to use "assessment data" to do interventions and differentiation to improve instruction. However when they *do* that, they are accused of skipping material or "dumbing down" regardless of how enriching and deep the activity is. Everyone at each level, principal, state inspectors, and for-profit school remediation companies, can't seem to allow the intervention because that would threaten their job. It never all comes together so even good teachers follow suit and just do what they're told.

In ten years, in this setting, with 110-120 students per year, I have not seen enough students with good attendance. This is a profoundly sobering statement. If this phenomenon could be illuminated, it would be possible to move forward with practical solutions. For the most part, this essential problem is swept to the margins. Respecting the integrity of everyone's life, the difficulty of sustained attendance is complicated. Analysis of the problem is none of my business. It will improve if individuals can problem-solve their own long term positive outcome, not a fix for a day.

The solution to almost every problem in urban education is "incentives." Prizes, candy, and cash are given for attendance, good grades, back-to-school night attendance, PTA meetings, and the apex of all wastelands: good behavior. Practitioners argue, "it shows them the love." Maybe, yes, maybe it just makes them dancing seals. It hurts to think about it. It hurts to think about how it sets kids up. Consider Alfie Kohn's book *Punished by Rewards*.

Every kid from second grade to fifth got a black T-shirt with yearly statistics of homicides in white, arranged attractively to look cool. This awesome gift was from the prosecutor's office and everyone loved them and thought it was a swell idea because kids would wear them and the concept would sink in dramatically. I don't have asthma, but I thought I was having an attack. I felt like I couldn't breathe. My fifth grade students knew the other classes got them. Mine were folded in a pile on a bookcase. A second day later, I was told to distribute them, I carried them folded down the stairs and in a perfectly cowardly act, handed them out, still folded, as the kids exited the building.

Life is a balancing act. Urban schools are full of great teachers and great students. Urban schools also have some challenged teachers and troubled students, just like suburban schools. Natural forces should have corrected these problems by 1995 or whenever the urban school outrage became loud. Funny that it never self-corrected and it's not correcting in the dictatorial testing climate. As mentioned above, it's now a lucrative industry managed by white, middle class, retired or "bailed-out" teachers and principals. Why would I respect someone who elects not to be in a classroom anymore? Why would I respect someone who retires at fifty-five, burdening other taxpayers and collecting another salary? The content of these "remedial" programs is never enlightening in any way to me, as a forty-year veteran and adjunct professor who teaches pedagogy; these programs are reductionist pablum.

Urban School Issues (Bullets)

Never-ending rollouts of "new" (recycled) programs

Absence of enriched curricula

Individual levels are ignored in the name of "rigor"

Candy

Attendance issues

Interruptions

Behavior modification instead of genuine cause and effect

Interruptions

Factors of poverty

Interruptions

Too many eye-glazing, boring practices

A percentage of exhausted or uninspired teachers

Budgets are admin/supervisor heavy

Interruptions

Pull-outs (guidance, gifted, music, speech, etc.) from major subjects

Interruptions

Too much testing and quizzing

Disregard for master teachers

Extreme disregard for one or more major American dialects

Volunteer

When you retire, you must volunteer. Think of economics in general. The basic balancing act of life systems makes this a requirement for world citizenship, planetary health, and the future of the children. Filling in the gaps (being careful not to eliminate paid work for job seekers) creates a manageable equilibrium for society. Apart from extreme weather and crazed dictators, the hum of the planet can be *steadied* with help from good people. This culture has too many gaps that need more mortar. There are two ways to think about service. Learning new skills is truly a selfish but wonderful benefit. Alternatively, doing things in which you are excellent, close to home, probably has a great bang for the societal buck. Consider your own family, friends, and neighbors.

You are an expert in this area. Consider schools, prisons, nature sanctuaries, and nonprofits. Use the Bayonne Nature Club as a model. These folks have created a paradise in an urban setting. They devote two to three days a week to native gardening in public parks, teaching others about wildlife, organizing massive clean-up days, and spreading an awesome amount of cheer. Use the Rockaway Valley Garden Club as another large scale model. They maintain a pristine Native Wildflower Trail among many other projects. Consider helping *deserving* start-up companies. Consider traveling to another continent where the suffering might be unquestionable.

Clean your storm drain. Go to the nearest park and pick up trash. Really.

War of Attrition

It's June and my "hard copy" attendance book has more cross-outs than a teacher would ever allow on a student's paper. I start the year skipping two spaces between each name and hope that I can at least get each new child in the right first-letter category. It almost never works out. Some years are worse than others. In 2006, my homeroom had every single September name crossed out and all new names were entered by June. It doesn't help that in sixth grade, which is the youngest in my middle school, guidance shuffles kids to better placements in mid-October, for many reasons. After I have hooked my students on gathering data on bees, or invasive species experiments, the students are suddenly in a different class. My team project is blown away to stunned speechlessness. How can a person score a passing grade with these circumstances? This gigantic problem could be improved with or without social scaffolding. One quick fix would be to teach very small self-contained units, shorter literary works, and smaller projects. I am sure there are other possible tactics for a semi-solution. The real fix is to pay guidance in August to do the right thing.

Waste of the Workhorse

I've never been even slightly interested in being a public school adminis-trator. Being a small private school administrator only worked for me because I was simultaneously a teacher, but I think I knew how to try to keep teachers a little happy by identifying their strengths and fostering settings that would promote those strengths.

In public school, I would volunteer one Saturday a season to hike with families in a designated location. I also came into the school all summer long to maintain two gardens. My colleague and I painted an outdoor mural one summer. We also volunteered to do many Saturday field trips by writing grants for transportation money. I volunteered to do weekly afterschool current events contests. And of course, there was volunteer gardening with students after school and sometimes before school. When we weren't gardening, we were just hanging out in my classroom full of weather stations, microscopes, telescopes, magnets, balance scales, and the daily caught creatures for after-noon release. In the gardening "off-season," we ran a drama club. This all was, of course, before the years of berserk testing.

Only three, out of many, administrators helped in any way: flyers, announcements, appreciation, including appreciation for subsidizing all of it. I will generously say that administrators in failing schools are putting out too many fires every day to notice anything.

When the "failing schools" grant, (School Improvement Grant), (S.I.G.) was bestowed upon us and we had additional "school" from 3:00–4:00 every day, all our real enrichment became defunct. The gardens became defunct as well.

We are at the Glorious Mercy of Our Teachers' Passions

Kids tune out their parents, but they have to at least pretend to be listening to their teachers. When a teacher is crazy about something, students notice, even if only in a quizzical way.

My sixth grade science teacher loved astronomy—funny thing, so do I. My third grade teacher loved Central American pre-Columbian history, and I find every Taino culture revelation at my emotional core.

A Sprout House student, Andrew R, corrected his parents on a weekend nature walk in what they thought was a Blue Jay was unconditionally a Kingfisher. He was six years old. His teacher, Mrs. Smallwood, provided so much outdoor experience that he knew it dynamically in the habitat, by sound, visual cues, and habit. Although he couldn't articulate it per se, it was an organic understanding. His parents, after quick research, realized their mistake and his accuracy.

I went through a period when I was obsessed with bridges. A student from those years has returned to tell me she is a bridge engineer.

Well ….Well …. Well ….April 2014

The first tests given to students, for the purpose of evaluating teachers has been given and graded. They are called SGOs. Something about Student Growth, I think. Oh, yes, Student Growth Objectives. We're madly recording data (instead of planning great lessons). But there's a glitch, a huge glitch. In my urban middle school, in my class, the "post-test" was taken by only 48 percent of the same students that took the pre-test. Only half the names are the same. Only half are still here. How does that measure my effectiveness, especially since I couldn't teach it the comprehensive and detailed way I needed to, because I had to teach the supervisor's "script" way. If the attendance problems weren't an issue, this would really be a metric of supervisor's effectiveness, if anything.

When All Else "Fails"

There's a certain secular spirituality that some teachers are able to summon up and drape over the integrity of their classrooms, making it a warm, fuzzy entity where kids can't go wrong. These giants of humanity can make a school setting that is *the* most rigid, reductionist, militant, workbook and standardized test mill, feel like a playground or good museum. If you're lucky, you have had at least one teacher like this in your life.

Ron Miller in "Reflecting on Spirituality in Education" *Encounter*, Summer, 2006, states, "a spiritual approach to education involves suspending our conceptual mindsets and standing in wonder and awe of life as it unfolds before us."

White Savior Complex

I'm glad I never heard about white savior complex (WSC) while I was volunteering to take kids on afterschool fossil-hunting trips and seining in the bay. When my teaching partner realized the bus wasn't going to show up one Saturday morning, he just walked over to the corner ATM and withdrew $450 to pay a different bus company on the spot. He and I never spoke of it. We would have been paralyzed if we knew it (WSC) was a "thing." That's a chilling shiver. I don't think it existed in my school. All teachers were outspokenly appreciative of us, as were certain administrators. I get that they had young kids and second jobs. I'm middle-aged with a husband who, bless his heart, loves to cook dinner. I'm just a science geek, who isn't interested in nail polish or clothes or shopping. Being with kids on adventures is what we like to do. Painting murals on school buildings in summer is what we like to do. When you know that their scores will go up unconsciously, and you and they are following the bliss, gardening with kids is what we like to do. I will, however, proudly accept "White Geek." Isn't volunteering what we're supposed to do when we can?

Why Are You an Administrator?

Really great teachers are brimming with ideas for activities. They like working with kids. They dream up activities at night, on the weekends, and on vacation. The percolation process happens automatically. The "breaking it down" process is a living, breathing animal. It's a car that's always running. It's what we do. It's our hobby. The thought of no paperwork at night (becoming an administrator) is very tantalizing, but we just can't slide down that slope. On the other hand, there are folks who become administrators who love the profession and want to crush all the stupid monsters by doing so in a big way. Control is not a dirty word here. They feel as though they can control a great big piece. Those folks are awesome.

Then there are the administrators who knew they would automatically make a six-digit salary usually with no night-time paperwork. A sometimes quiet office, instead of being in a room for six periods with twenty other exuberant humans, is a draw. There are no painful report cards to write.

Who Eats Whales?

Why can't I just sail into the sunset (retire quietly) of the bombastic setting we call public education? In my last week, there is no shortage of incidents. This is the time when the individuality, cuteness, cleverness, and humor of middle schoolers should be making me explode with regret. Alternately, I am crawling to the finish line, hoping that I don't die from reacting wrongly, falling on glass science equipment, or getting run over in the hallways. I have lost so many colleagues in the past five years. They had health issues but were coming to work with no problem. Then there would be a day when they went home, sat in a chair, or went to bed normally and never got up. It's difficult to find an employee who doesn't think the job killed a person who would have otherwise lived a much longer life.

It's the end of year and this district has a policy of giving finals five to ten days before the end of the year. The kids know we can change a grade or two after that but we can't change every grade.

In this post-finals time of year, we were having a lovely day in a particular class, which contains at least three unruly students. It was, in fact, a miracle. We were playing science games in the context of the unit on "Common Ancestor," in other words *evolution.* Various groups were studying adaptations of species within the genus. One group had crabs of NJ. Another had birds of NJ, whales migrating past NJ, and so on. They had card-size pictures with which to do an activity. Everything was going well, really well. I was summoned by the group with the whales that migrate twice a year past NJ. A female student, who normally does homework, is sweet, focused, and helpful with a C average is in the whale group. Her three group-mates are laughing with their hands covering their mouths. Two of the suppressed laughers are extremely shy and quiet individuals. The "summoner" is pointing to one species and asks me, "Ms. White, who eats sperm?" I ignored it. She asked it again. I then said, "Excuse me?" She repeats it a third time while my anger at this profound disrespect goes through the roof. I respond, "We're doing adaptations, not the food chain, but I will call your mom and ask her if she knows the answer. I will also ask her if she knows why you would ask that question in science class when we're studying adaptations, not the food chain." She protests that she should be able to ask science questions. I respond, "You make your decisions and I make mine." The home phone number did not work so I told her to take a note home asking for a way to reach her parent. She was calm and compliant.

After school, I was told by the next teacher that the student cried from 1:25 until 4:00 p.m.

The next morning I consulted with her homeroom teacher who characterized her as very "sneaky." I had never seen that side, but it's not unusual for kids to present differently to different teachers.

When I should be using my lunchtime to pack up my closets because I am parting ways with this school and district, I am in a tribunal with the assistant principal and two guidance counselors because my whale scholar has not returned the note from her parent. Her version of the story is that she asked me, "Who eats whales?"

Why Fireworks?

Why do American humans adore fireworks? It brings neighbors together. It brings strangers together. They're pretty and sort of thrilling. Hmm ….not very when you think about it. Is it a cosmic remembering? Is it a left over vestige of loving stars and meteors? Perhaps. It's got to be. There's no other explanation for something so wasteful and expensive. Certainly American wildlife and domestic animals recoil at the sensation.

An urban school could go on twenty overnight field trips to marine biology outposts or stargazing trips with the donated money of one suburban town giving up fireworks for one year. I'm obsessed with some kind of "freakonomics."

Why I Am a Good Teacher

I am a good teacher because 10 out of 10 times, I ask the questions kids would ask. I think like a kid. I zero in on the heart of the matter like a kid and in the same order as a kid. An MRI of my brain would show similar shapes in neuron-branching to an adolescent. I can't think of any other explanation for this ostentatious bravado and bluster.

With Limited Experience ("Developmentally Appropriate Curriculum")

With limited life experience, high school seniors declare majors for their college applications. I chose French. Loved it, got straight A's and figured it would lead to travel opportunities. One of my great-grandparents was Quebecois. My father used French phrases (for fun) that his live-in grandmother had used with him.

Fast forward a few months. During college orientation, I took the French placement exam. I scored into a very high course. French 7—whatever that meant. My dorm neighbor scored into French 5, both of us having taken four years of high school French; I fell flat on my face. I got a devastating grade of C. She got an A. My spirit, interest and confidence flat-lined. She graduated with a Language degree.

This shouldn't have happened. Despite my strong background and resiliency, I was a flop. I fell between the proverbial cracks. The kids with tougher baggage might not be able to rally. Luckily, I did. Similar in many ways, the AP (Advanced Placement) hype sometimes results in the same syndrome, according to researchers at prestigious schools. The problem is that you don't get into those schools without AP courses.

Workload and Extra Forty-Five minutes

The moment is in October 2014. We are sitting in a faculty meeting with a very nice new principal who talks to us respectfully.

Our "failing school" has opted for a certain plan of action in order to avoid a state takeover.

The following plan is bigger than she is. She is just part of the pecking order. There are mandatory cross-curricular assignments for science teachers. All subject area teachers have similar workloads.

To our amazement, we are told that the school day will increase by forty-five minutes starting September 2015. I gasp because I am behind in the requirements (see Job Description) and I have no evenings or weekends because of those requirements. Where would the time come from for additional mandates and the accompanying paperwork? I remind myself that a few teachers have died in my building over the past few years. I can only assume that although there were medical reasons, the outcomes were stress-related. Many people in the building have these concerns.

A few ideas can possibly solve this dilemma:

1. Bring in outside professionals to deliver exciting SKILL-oriented programs such as bicycle mechanics, cooking, sewing, industrial arts, etc. According to ALL brain research, skills transform into brain power. My garden club students always pass the eighth grade science test, Language Arts Literacy(LAL), and math tests.

OR

2. Reduce the amount of busy work loaded on to the teachers so that they can deliver these programs themselves. I would be interested in providing an afterschool entomology program. Keep in mind that any truly interesting program that requires more than paper, pencil, and computer will require SET UP TIME and CLEAN

UP TIME and these need to be factored into the plan by reasonable administrators.

By the way, those extra forty-five minutes? That was part of the School Improvement Grant (SIG) that year. By its own admission, several years later, there was "no significant impact on math or reading scores, high school graduation, or college enrollment." The nationwide bill was close to $7 billion. In most districts, SIG was delivered as reductionist tutoring.

World Citizenship

Education is nothing if the most important lesson isn't one of world citizenship. My dear friend, Ingrid, used to say to me, "We'll never have world peace if we can't get along at home." So kids getting along with classmates and teachers is step one. How to do that? Stay engaged in unquestionably interesting activities, activities where you "lose" yourself and don't hurt anything else in doing so. Help other classes with their activities. Then help other schools with theirs. Help your neighbors. Be part of the community. Reach out to sister communities. Even in the Olympics, you can't help but see how the athletes admire each other and form highly respected bonds.

Anyone over fifty has seen all kinds of relationships at home, at work, and in the neighborhood. These fifty-somethings have also seen a phenomenon where they know two parties who are having a conflict. They love both and listen to both sides. Each has a strong, positive reality. How can that be? It's mathematically impossible to hear both sides and be unable to synthesize this strange energy. In my decades worth of troubleshooting, I often can see the two reasonable scenarios. The quandary of the Palestinians and the Israelis is a heartbreaking example. It's our job to try to penetrate bubbles like these, no matter how intangible, or, at least, somehow support each side. It's part of being busy with positive activities. Think of the camp, Seeds of Peace, which takes Israeli and Palestinian children in the summer; there are very small and very large pieties at the same time.

Carrying the ethical responsibility of weighing actions against what's good for everybody is the understated teacher turf. Everybody, of course means all things and soil, bedrock, air; you name it...

Writing Samples

For the most part, this society does not take an impromptu, unprepared writing sample from college applicants, but does do it to fourth graders on their state tests.

Wrong Direction

Internalized, self-motivated learning seems to be gasping its last breath. The trumpets are blasting packaged, data-accessible school experiences. Google Classroom will allow a teacher to   assign a project with a rubric.... (and the teacher) can post an exemplar along with it for students to have an idea of what they are striving for. After all that effort on the part of the teacher, you can be sure that only 20 percent of the teachers will actually have enough energy to make it an interesting project. More than likely, it will boil down to something like: "Create a day in the life of a girl from Mesopotamia." Nothing wrong with that, but it leaves much less time for hands-on, primary-source learning. Not to *mention* teachable moments that can morph into authentic lesson plans, such as the meteor shower or eclipse last night, the geothermal wells being installed next door or the northern brown snake den discovered under the girls' locker room.

Google Classroom will also make it easier for students to see a week's worth of assignments, classwork, and homework. What's wrong with that? Learning is no longer a living, breathing experience. It's locked in place. There's no stopping for a great current events happening. There's no branching off in a tangent for one or more self-directed, motivated students. There's no speeding up for more advanced scholars. There's no space for the teacher to incorporate a last minute brainstorm. It's a locked system. There's no way to deal with having to stop for a social-emotional problem, unannounced assembly, fire drill, you name it. These things are the norm in some schools. Did I mention that it's locked in place? If you can say to a teacher, "My child will be absent for one week next month because we need to go to City X, please give me his assignments," and the teacher can indeed print them out in seconds, know that that program could be deader than all doornails. Wrong direction.

Student of the week, month, year is a platform for teachers and administrators who can't quite teach or administer. They can't quite get kids to internally motivate themselves. It screams: "I can't come up with anything else." Resorting to contests is the wrong direction. You have failed to spark.

If Google Classroom is the digital platform that demonstrates rigidity, God help us understand the genesis of Dojo. Dojo makes George Orwell's ideas look like a charming, bucolic, family picnic. Dojo digitally alerts parents by text of behavior credits all day long. Not only that, but the student's other teacher's computers are "notification-buzzing" all over the building with every good and not-so good event in that child's day. I have 115 students. Imagine what that's like as background noise. Also imagine what it's like to input all these students and enjoy all the little cutesy avatars. Imagine how much fun it is to change, when the guidance counselors reshuffle the classes in October (a sixth grade phenomenon, or whatever class is youngest to the building) and adding and removing all the students who transfer and return, not to mention the new admissions. The darling avatars just swirl in my head.

Avoid the underlying problems and develop time-consuming Band-Aids. Someone is always getting credit for inventing a product that treats symptoms instead of causes. Wrong direction.

You Can't Be Nice? Being Nice Didn't Work

My dear friend Claire used to say about a certain person, "You can't be nice (to him)." What kind of a way is that to live? He would *sometimes* psychologically abuse her and she came to that conclusion, despite the fact that he was most often very good to her. Claire, to me, was one of the most perfect human beings. Mother Teresa is "here," and Claire is slightly above.

I sort of understood her point, but also unfortunately lived it for two months as a new teacher in a middle school setting.

My kind of "nice" involves sense of humor and really getting to know each individual person and trying to relate to them in as genuine a way as best I can, with over one hundred individuals a day. (Oh, and teach a major subject.) Being fair is a big part of being nice. Included in that, trying to put yourself in their shoes in a big way.

After my first month of being nice, not saccharine nice, not dopey nice, and not "second chance" nice, just fair/warm nice, there were a few times that I felt like the object of disrespect. In the beginning, my homeroom students came close to ten minutes late every day. One or two disregarded every verbal instruction, a few hurtful tricks such as glue in my coffee cup and one incident of hilarious, but disgusting vandalism. Although it was decidedly a minute percentage of the whole group, it was wonderful drama for the rest to enjoy. This all made the first two months of that year quite unpleasant. I won them back with phone calls home, dedicated problem-solving with the mischievous initiators, and some awesome field trips. I was lucky. A small quantity of exacting rules were bedrock as well.

Being fair with rules is the same as being nice because there is still the positive regard, sense of humor, and getting to know all those interesting personalities. Again for whatever reason, a certain small group doesn't look like it accepts the reality of good work and getting along. This results in drama and the profound power of a performance for the others, who are thrilled to watch the show.

The drama is a big problem because the huge majority are radiant, clever, friendly, and interesting kids. But screaming and laughing all the way, they will stampede down a flight of stairs if they hear there is a fight on the second floor.

Of course, another logical solution was for science teachers to volunteer to lead an invigorating, afterschool drama club.

You Can't Put People in a Room and Do Nothing

Move symbols all day? Maybe for a worthy goal ….
but not all day
Frozen bodies in furniture. That's too severe. That's too
Long….how long?
Long as a river that seems unending but always manages to find the
estuary.
Forty minutes is forty minutes….even with the
gimmicks.
The gimmicks are not life….eye-glazing as the symbols, maybe
worse in their
deceit.
For lack of meaning, our self-respect guides us to be actors, sometimes bad
actors.
Worst of all the lovely carrots that bury our sacredness deeper than
carrots could ever be ….and one cell does not reach out to another.

You Can't Hold Me Accountable

You can't hold me accountable for my students not hitting "the mark"
when you've bullied me into your curriculum, your program, your style, your
delivery, your objectives, your scope and sequence, your criticisms, your
books, your censorship of the internet, your lack of a budget, your tests and
quizzes, your lesson plan critiques, and your state testing.

You can't hold me accountable for a Smartboard curriculum and
no Smartboard.

You can't hold me accountable for your script, then the next script, and
the next…..

CURRICULUM

A Four-Foot Neuron!

One of my favorite lessons, which I plan for the first or second day of fifth or sixth grade, is the assignment to draw an 8½ x 11-inch neuron. We talk about the beautiful branching and connectivity possibilities, skinny neurons compared to plumper ones. Taking care of neurons and increasing their numbers and size is researched by everyone, then shared in small groups. We talk about how the chemicals must jump from one to another if the neurons are not close or connected. We talk about reasons why neurons grow or don't grow, and why they might not attach or slip apart after being attached.

The second part of the lesson is a large, in-your-face constant reminder: a neuron, which is poster- or mural-size, rendered by anyone who is willing to come after school to donate their art skills.

This activity is frowned upon by the science supervisor because it is not part of the (his) curriculum, and I quote from his written displeasure, "you cannot unilaterally create curriculum; please adhere to the pacing guide." He also writes that comment when I am caught teaching science current events in science.

It's also hard to conceal a four-foot neuron.

Action Research

Meaningful Work: First hand research is authentic work. It makes sense for kids to study their neighborhood. Of interest are things that live there and the interactions of all the systems there, biological, social, economic, and political.

For example, here's a list a fifth grade class of mine wrote in 2007.

We identify bird species in the neighborhood.

We count numbers of individual species at migration time.

We tally behaviors.

We diagram the position of the sun through the year.

We learn to use the tools of research.

We graph data that relates to us (like daily temperature averages).

We find answers that we need from many sources.

We scan the news sources every day for information that shouldn't be missed. We tally things of individual interest.

We count invertebrates within a square meter in the vacant lot.

We graph the number of daylight hours through the seasons.

We survey opinions of friends and family (i.e. What do you think is the greatest benefit of trees? Have you ever gone fishing? How many ways can you cook eggs? How many birds in the neighborhood can you name? Where is the nearest storm drain to your house?)

Adaptively Attuned

Aaron James, University of California, professor of Philosophy at Irvine, has written a book, I can only assume, for me to make my point that school needs to be organic. Just kidding. Schooling can't be a stale, pre-ordained, crusty, obligatory, national curriculum, written 1–5 years previous(ly) by strangers. *Surfing With Sartre* (Doubleday, 2017) uses the compelling metaphor of a contemplative, solitary sport. When a wave does "this," you must do "that." Surfing is the quintessential, immediate, constant, problem-solving exercise.

Aaron James improves on Mr. Sartre's metaphor for *freedom* in skiing. James uses the liquid form of H2O being even more awesomely pliable in fluid, for surfing. Freedom is a prerequisite of deep learning. Hence, surfing tests the brain cells only with access to complete freedom in decision-making. The whole process reeks of intimate trust in one's own neurons. Aaron James calls it "adaptively attuned," otherwise known more or less, as sensorimotor intelligence, constructivism, zone of proximal development, wild schooling, essential questions, and more. For the most part, this education phenomenon never becomes widespread, even with tiny pockets of great success. Perhaps this book will stir the pot.

I love the phrase "adaptively attuned" because it shows a oneness with changing conditions. Life is just a string of circumstances and moving targets. Children who are adaptively attuned won't just be looking to get through the homework; they will relish it if they are accustomed to a rich backdrop of substantial, real-life materials.

Which project would you like to do? (Examples)

1. Track, map, and collect data of monarch migration this year.

2. Count and describe and research nests in a city park in winter

3. Sketch, research, and map the schoolyard trees.

James says you must change something about yourself to stay up on the surfboard with each nuance of wave physics, and be conscious of the intention to participate.

That's just scholarship.

Continuous reassessment is also, of course, the hallmark of great teachers, not just great students.

Adult Failures

The learning issues of troubled school systems are defyingly complex. There's eagerness on the part of the children, but there are difficulties with retention, retention meaning "memory retention." Eagerness is disregarded which is crushing in every way. There are attendance and punctuality issues. It's hard to master things when some weeks you come to school for four days. On standardized tests, in measuring comprehension, there is not always much to relate to in terms of content or vocabulary. Listening to fifth graders read aloud, you realize that almost no one stops at the end of a sentence. There's major pain in putting a grammatically correct, standard English sentence on the line. Administrators ignore the fact that a beautiful and precise, but completely different dialect predominates.

Many children are transferred from one school to another often for various reasons. I sometimes only have a few of the same students in June that I had in September. I've noticed an interesting phenomenon. New students have an amazing capacity for figuring out the lay of the land in one swallow. The names of the administrators, the locations of all school offices, all the stairways, the schedule, the bathrooms, the cool teachers, the uncool teachers, cafeteria rules, how the school works and all the names in the class—that's a lot to process and it's done flawlessly. A lot of skills have to intersect to accomplish that much learning. Scores are low because of adults' failures…. not kids'.

Be on the Planet

Most people insulate themselves in a sanitary, clinical artificial existence. *Hidden Heart of the Cosmos* by Brian Swimme is one of the works that made me get back on a planet. I went to work in a metal box, got food out of a large building, transformed it in a smaller metal box with dials, put a rubber-material garment around myself when the atmosphere was less than dry, watched stories on a screen, talked to friends through a plastic implement, and listened to music electronically. Despite all my truly live activities (going to the beach, gardening, stargazing, hiking, raising butterflies, etc.), I had to learn to be *ON* the planet. Good teachers can do this.

Brian Swimme instructs us to watch a sunset imagining being on a huge ball rolling back. It's a whole different perception.

Columbus

At Sprout House in the late '80s, I didn't even bring it up to the board of directors; I just told the office administrator, Pat, that I felt uncomfortable calling a holiday Columbus Day, **especially** since I am 50 percent Italian-American. Our social studies curriculum was layered in primary sources, such as visits to every local historical location. Jockey Hollow, Chatham's main street, beehive ovens in town, the Boisoban House, Miller Cory House, Fort Nonsense, Washington's Headquarters, Washington Rock to only name a few that were part of our weekly field trips. Disrespecting many history "textbooks" produced by large corporations, we used the Joy Hakim narrative stories for framework instead. Accurate literary, nonfiction was plentiful. Students liked history a lot.

No one asked any questions when the school calendar came out and it said: October 12, North America Day.

I just couldn't think of a better phrase. It was interesting that there was no discussion.

Corporate Literary Junk

I have often watched late night TV to see the host's perspective on the news for that day. Sometimes I even stay past the monologue. Too often I am surprised that such smart and clever, people, when interviewing people with children, will collectively discuss their own children's toys. The sadness just squeezes the air out of me that these people and their smart celebrity guests' children worship at the altar of corporate toy characters from movies and TV shows. It's obvious that they are employed by these corporations but I wish they discussed other pastimes. I feel so sad when children are not gravitating to characters rendered in pure art.

I used to tell new teachers at Sprout House and my graduate students, "If a figurine/toy was crafted by a corporate team, it can't come to Sprout House: If there is no author of a children's book, don't bring it in the building." Yes, call it controlling and micromanaged censorship on my part. The honestly sick feeling in my stomach makes me wonder if the team of corporate creators actually bring this stuff home to their own offspring. I doubt it.

Current Events

What is the subject that is seldom taught in school? When I taught fifth grade, my students were "in the flow" (Mihalyi Csikszentmihalyi) I didn't want them to be "left behind." They knew who Al Gore was and that he had a chance of winning a Pulitzer Prize. They knew that he worked for England! They knew what a Pulitzer was and they knew where England was! They knew local news stories as well. They knew who their congressperson was and their senators, and state senators! They talked about local officials and we wrote them notes and letters, a lot. They lived and breathed being part of something small and also something bigger.

The little chirpy "automatons" who know their eight times table for the state test, but forget it by the next September are not in the flow.

There is an eerie reluctance to even approaching the real world by classroom teachers. It is the number one most important item kids can attend to. I am referring to "current events."

A meteorite fell through a house. Twenty-nine out of thirty teachers in my school ignored it. A woman became Speaker of the House. It was the teachable moment for the three branches of government for all middle schoolers, maybe younger. A new Secretary General took his position at the United Nations. Most students were in the dark.

Starting in fourth grade, students would do well to have face recognition with world leaders and their local leaders. Who are our state representatives?

Who are our national representatives? Who is the mayor? What are their stories? One picture leads to another, and the teacher's interest in these elevated individuals compels the young student to notice. If not, it becomes an overwhelming jumble to learn it later. Tuning out is what is done when levels of understanding start stacking up and it becomes harder to understand your world. This mountain of incomprehensible jargon is a eulogy for the ability to catch up as an authentic citizen. It's a eulogy for the triggers to acquire the symbolic tools for understanding the world. Students then lower the bar for intellectually sophisticated activities and seek other activities to make them feel happy and fulfilled, perhaps complicated in their own right, but not necessarily advancing them academically.

It goes without saying that students from underrepresented groups will benefit by nurturing curiosity about bigger than life personalities and issues.

Being informed makes you a player. Players need tools whether they are just good communication skills or electrical power tools. When you are a player, you will be motivated to put yourself in interesting situations. Interesting situations will inspire you to do more. Interesting situations hook you into wanting and needing more background. All these branching networks translate into "information fluency." When you can manipulate facts, systems start to make more sense. Problem solving improves by shear ability to mentally manipulate facts and systems. There is more than a small chance using these abilities will help you to think metaphorically because when small facts make sense in larger and larger systems, complete understandings can be transposed and applied to new scenarios. Having *authentic* information, that is information *in context,* builds a mental repertoire (reliably solid branching dendrites and terminal fibers) to support the leaps to creativity, innovative thinking, decision-making, and problem-solving.

The ultimate assault on our American students is that current events aren't in the formal curriculum very often. You will understand this immediately if you ever watched Jay Leno interviewing people on the street. Most don't know what's going on in their world and they therefore find it difficult to remember the facts of the same world years and years ago.

In my school setting, it goes without saying, that I have had points taken off my evaluations for deviating from the curriculum by spending a few minutes on the events of the day which, of course, is insubordinate.

For a middle school science teacher, it is imperative that every new science discovery is available to students. Every shred of science news should be considered and illuminated for students in an age-appropriate way. Perhaps briefly and to the point.

Current Events is not a subject but a framework that should embrace all the subjects like the curvature of space-time.

As an addendum, covering current events opens up the drama of inappropriate stories. I openly advocate benevolent censorship. Social studies teachers should be covering civics stories, math teachers must follow economics, language arts teachers human interest stories. Feel no remorse about censoring the raunchy, sensational, or violent. And leave your politics at home, which I struggle with every day.

Cursive.... Worse-ive

Next to getting your very own locker, the second best thing about reductionist schools is learning cursive writing, or at least the anticipation of it. But maybe I should say that was two decades ago. The teaching of cursive writing is almost gone and it wasn't phased out thoughtfully. It was axed to make room for computer classes. As a fifth grade teacher, I loved teaching cursive because I could see that everyone looked forward to it. Since those groups in 2007 and 2008 were victims of "the axe" in the third or fourth grade, I surreptitiously taught it in fifth grade. It was a relaxing period where spelling and sentence structure could be reinforced without tyranny. Spelling and sentence structure! This is an effortless way to remedy one of the bigger buggers of education and test scores and it's totally ignored. Practicing and reinforcing those "ea" phonics was a valuable moment. I created sentences about my students for them to copy. They were the stars of the texts. It was just a tiny bit more labor for me. Even a store-bought learning system would reinforce easy spelling and grammar without shame.

Now fast forward to middle school where teachers born in the '60s, '70s, or '80s write on a Smartbooard or chalkboard in cursive. Imagine how disastrously lost that makes a student because they can't decipher it.

No matter how technological a society becomes, there will always be a need to handwrite something. Students who "make up" their own form of cursive end up having spelling criticism because the o's turn into a's; the q's turn into g's, etc. often.

There is a curious lack of discussion on this phenomenon in the education community.

Designing Worksheets

Brain research (and common sense) tells us that after kids complete their tenth math problem or tenth grammar problem, they zone out. I have found that three of the same kind of problem is the limit for good practice, UNLESS, it is about them, your own students. Word problems with *their own name or class's* activities mentioned in the question. I got into the habit of designing a grammar page with five to ten sentences almost every day about our class.

Language Arts:

Underline the subject once. Underline the verb twice.

"The sycamore, outside our classroom window, has a nest."

"We counted five monarchs at recess yesterday."

"We will see if our beetles are attracted to the apple slice."

Math:

If Alexis and Angel needed to babysit to pay for a camp deposit that cost $18 each, how many hours would they each need to work at $4 per hour?

Now there's nothing wrong with using textbook examples some of the time, but practitioners capable of deep teaching will throw in relevance because relevant examples are all around.

Early Childhood Training....for Middle School Teachers?

Early Childhood teacher training is an imposing mindset for genuinely educating middle school teachers!

Give them options. Give them learning centers. Move their muscles. Let them *construct* knowledge. Meet them where they are. Respect half-steps of knowledge. Take them outside. Let them get dirty. Have a chat! Engage in active listening. Have a sing-along. Read a story together. Act it out. Bake bread.

Event Mentality

The circus concept has come and gone, but not before many, many people and other living things were exploited.

Scheduling in defiance of normal, healthful rhythms of living and learning is stressful. Notice the bribing of seals to dance and ponies to perform or carry unusual objects. Attention show-offs of the world acting for the sake of profound or subtle pay-offs. Attention !.

Events are what the creative-challenged resort to when school-life is not content-rich. I do know that some folks plan events out of love. I would kindly urge some focus on developing quieter, integrated richness.

Harmful? Sometimes. Vacuous? Usually. Time-waster? You decide.

An event can have substance if you are satisfied with the event's purpose. What is the purpose of your Event?

Field Trips

Field trips to the outdoors are vivid and vital labs. This is my favorite teaching activity; it is a courtship of contentment and accidental rhythm.

I usually go with only a minor objective. Exceptions would be things like a quest to see the horseshoe crab/shorebird migration in Cape May on the full moon in May, or snake emergence in Great Swamp the third week of March.

See "OBJECTIVES" and Jargon. Going with only a *tiny* objective on a nature-type trip is contrary to every lesson (and format) developed in the past twenty years. Perhaps this is mandated because some of the adults masquerading as teachers are not truly dedicated professionals, and/or that teachers as a group have not won the confidence of the general public. Either way, those amusing requirements are meant to teach us a lesson. Disregard those pompous objectives for the outdoor field trip.

Once you get there, focus on and absorb what is there.

Another teacher and I went to a very local park, which happens to be the design work of Frederick Law Olmstead. It's an arboretum because he went all over the world to find various specimens. (He thought he was doing a good thing.) We went to study the trees. We sat down for a picnic lunch and were stunned as monarch butterflies floated over us at regular intervals, about every three minutes heading south in September, of course. We counted eighteen before we moved on to another activity. It takes a lot to mesmerize students who are revved up for a field trip. Put all your eggs in the butterfly basket!

When you are leading an outdoor field trip, you will be worrying about the weather for the previous 48 hours. You will have to decide when and if to cancel. You will need to have the thick kind of garbage bags and scissors to transform them into raincoats if you do get caught. On my worst weather disaster, the kids loved designing their raincoats (unexpected consequence), but it rained so hard that we got drenched anyway, a tornado appeared, then a fanciful rainbow and a crystal-clear sky. I don't recommend taking chances with other people's children, but you sometimes have to think on your toes.

Then there are mosquitoes. They love to sabotage outdoor field trips. I bring catnip toys for the kid with the mosquito-attracting chemistry and lots of garlic cloves to rub behind our knees and elbows. I give students crushed fresh basil or mint for their pockets. I spray DEET on shoes and perhaps clothing, *never* skin.

If you are not well-versed in outdoor activities, focus on size, shape, color, and connections. Download trail maps. Splash in a stream if it's hot (wear old shoes). Be very educated in poison ivy. Analyze the topography and the rocks. Be sure to visit first without students. Keep the groups small. Give chaperones a short list of rules.

One of my extreme favorite activities is using two small buses for two classes. One starts at the trailhead with a teacher and chaperone. The other class starts at the trail end with the other teacher and another chaperone. They meet in the middle for lunch. They proceed to the other bus and take the other bus back to school. The minute the groups meet is mysteriously hilarious and uplifting.

Outdoor Field Trips can be quests, but as in the preliminary caution, quests can be a jinx, so keep the goals flexible. Take the pulse of the group, watch for signs of fear or hypothermia. Always carry a tiny spray bottle of water for heat relief or first aid.

Always follow these three rules:

Count heads

Count heads

Count heads

Leave before they want to go home.

Flow vs. Bullying: Common Core Curriculum Standards

The kids are blissfully "lost" in the monarch caterpillars' constant hunger, transforming leaves into poop, or "frass." They are generating facts, questions, applications, and contrasts to other species without prompting! Every core curriculum standard bullied into their heads in the textbook is, instead, effortlessly secured in their neurons through the meaningful work of raising monarch butterflies.

First you learn to identify the genus host plant that monarch caterpillars need to eat. Kids can do that so easily. It's right outside. Our particular species is considered a weed, which is a completely different, but important lesson. Our plentiful habitat for this species is a vast laboratory for students to exercise their skills of discrimination as they look for monarch eggs. When I teach physical properties of matter later on in the year I review how specific that little egg was. There are so many other life forms in this milkweed community, but the monarch egg is singular. It's pale yellow, football-shaped with lines like football stitching and only 2 mm long. The total milkweed populations are a balanced microcosm, the nuances of which hold formidable learning potential.

The supervisor (in this school system) can't fathom this project-based focus. There's his way or nothing. His way consists of a new concept every day and nothing else (objective-lesson-closure). He doesn't know my 110 students or me, obviously and yet he can decide with arrogant conviction what my lessons should look like. There's obviously no embarrassment for his imperious micromanaging where it's not needed. Where it IS needed, bullying by any other name, is not the answer.

Forcing Ten-Year-Olds to Write Poetry (or anything for that matter)

Being an author, or the desire to be an author, is a profound experience. You have to really have something to say to the world, or at least a segment of the population. That's not what being ten years old is about. Being ten is about building go-carts, (yes, even screens-addicted ten-year-olds will slowly smile at the possibility of such a project), learning to use a telescope, building a campfire, climbing a great tree, body surfing, baking cookies from scratch, painting a historic mural, etc.) They want to *construct*, transform, or play rather than lecture or fabricate an intricate story, however much they love to hear stories.

The coercion, or bullying, that goes on with the elementary and middle school group, is widespread. There might be a handful of intrinsic "writers" but for the most part, a polite, medicinal sigh will then produce some sort of essay. Failing language arts scores are the proof here. I can still remember as a high school student in the '60s the same feeling. NOW even younger children get to feel that frustration.

How much mediocre poetry can be hung on a fifth grade bulletin board? Fine for the individuals who enjoy writing it. Torture for those of us who have to pretentiously show enthusiasm for it. What messages have the writers been given?

Straightforward, fourth grade journal-writing is literally the most earnest music without the intimidating coercion of "format." The trailer is ahead of the tractor heading for a collision with blissful learning. Poetry springs from experience with life and an attraction to wordplay.

Reading great age-appropriate poetry is fitting and captivating. Admitting the show-off potential of the "poetry" bulletin boards is essential.

Gimmicks

When classroom activity is not driven by meaningful, purposeful learning, an industry can and has blossomed to keep kids active with gimmicks. This, of course, is a yawn for the "crap detecting" kids. However insulting I am to these strategies, I will concede that they ARE fun once in a blue moon only as a diagnostic or review. These routines push organic learning backwards because these routines are meant to activate dead factoids. When they become a habit, kids are getting the message that life is one long snore-fest. There are also plenty of behavior abuses possible (ample time to trip others, poke others, install chewed gum in various locations, etc.). The mediocrity that these activities promote is almost worse than bad teaching. This is an outgrowth of well-meaning developers in the 1980s trying to move forward from teachers constantly lecturing. It was originally called "Cooperative/ Collaborative Learning Strategies."

These are the names of just some of the currently, so-called "Active" Learning Strategies:

1. Think-Pair-Share (Students think quietly about possible answers to a question. Then they pair with a learning buddy to discuss their thinking. Share responses with a larger group.)

2. Corners (A question is posed with multiple answers. Each corner of the room is designated for each possible answer. Students go to the corner of the room with those who share their opinion.

In the corner, the reasons for the answer are discussed among those students.)

3. Inside-Outside Circles: Students form two concentric circles, making pairs that face each other. The inner circle has questions for the person they are facing in the outer circle. After a certain number of minutes, the inner circle moves and they repeat with another person.

4. I Have the Question . . . Who Has the Answer? Students in groups are given answer cards. A pack of question cards are placed face down on the table. Questions are read. Correctly identifying their "answer," a student will gain points.

5. Graffiti Students are given questions, markers, and post-its. Divided into groups, each group gets a different question to be answered on the post-it. The groups trade post-its and thoughtfully answer the next question until all questions are thoroughly covered.

6. Formulas, problems, translations, brainstorming concepts, etc. are written on large pieces of paper and posted around the room. Students move singly or in groups around the room to write their answers or opinions.

7. Frame of Reference: A picture of a concept or a phrase is written in the center of a paper or piece of cardboard. Individually, or in a group, words or phrases are written in the area around the central concept framing that idea. This brainstorming is then shared with the larger group.

8. Consensus Conclusions: Individually, students generate the most important three facts on a given topic. Students gather in small groups. They share their own three facts and filter all lists to make a group list of the most important facts.

9. Biography in a Bag (A team of students study one topic and contribute "artifacts" on the topic to the bag.)

10. Consensogram (For self-esteem building, a topic is the title of a page. On the far left column, the top line reads 100 percent, the

second line 90 percent all the way down to zero. Many of these small posters are displayed around the classroom. Students walk around with sticky notes and attach one next to the percentage that represents how much they know about the topic.)

11. Connection Collections Objects or pictures are drawn from bags that relate to the course of study. Students make written or verbal predictions about the meaning of the object.

12. So-called poems. Every line answers a certain question and voila, it's a poem.

13. Learning Links (Teacher provides a list of key concepts. On another sheet of paper, students take notes from their textbooks etc. to make clusters of info. Students graphically display material with some kind of unique chart)

14. Stir the Class (my favorite). Each student gets a data collection sheet. Each student writes three comments about the topic to be studied. At the signal, students move around the room collecting items from others' lists. They then return to their seats to prioritize the list.

15. Graphic organizers. Any simplified chart of patterns that can be generated by students or filled in by students. This can involve folded mini-posters or varied diagrams. The ancestor is the famous diagrammed sentence.

16. Gots and Needs. On a sticky-note with their name, students write a quick note about what they "got" in the lesson or what they still "need" to understand. As they exit the class, they put the sticky note on the appropriate wall area for each.

17. Web (Graph a concept with facts emanating outward.)

Using these activities sparingly has a vastly different effect from when they are used comprehensively. Some teachers are encouraged to use these like it was a religion in the name of "hands-on" learning. Let's say kids are sophisticated enough to do these trite activities. At that level, wouldn't it be better to pursue primary documents or primary experiences like researching a native (weed) plant outdoors with all the accompanying invertebrate life on it? The contrived activities get kids physically moving but they consume a huge amount of time. Kids with good crap-detecting skills will tire. When used generously, it misses the whole point of education being real. You be the judge.

Ignoring Dinosaurs

If aliens came to our planet a hundred million years ago, they would have found a lush world with a remarkably diverse order of animals. The dominant terrestrial animal ranged in magnitude from seventy tons to hummingbird-size, with over seven hundred species. Many of these were twenty feet or larger. If those same aliens came again to our planet now, they would find the dominant terrestrial species was on average five feet, relatively hairless, with such large brains requisite adaptations have prevailed. This dominant species likes to transform materials, and the stunningly changed look of the planet would demonstrate that fact.

The profound transformation of who runs the planet is ignored by the education establishment. It's an essential concept that can be studied by middle school and high school students. In my state and many others, dinosaurs do not make it into the curriculum, except for enrichment by creative teachers at the peril of veering away from what's going to show up on "the exam." The most unique scientific condition that rivets young minds is almost totally ignored.

Contemplate the setting of the popular 2009 movie *Avatar*. The fictional planet was of course, a metaphor for Earth. The wildlife on Earth has been no less stunning in range and complexity as those in the movie. As we watch the compelling richness of the planet diminishing, shouldn't our offspring capture every nuance? At the risk of using current education-jargon, shouldn't dinosaurs be the greatest "hook" of all?

Keep the Ball in the Air

One of the great perils of "modern" thinking about learning is the lack of use. Children on traditional farms really understand earth science because they apply weather to success or failure, over and over. Meteorological concepts frame everything. They understand the texture of astronomy as they plot in their minds, the time of the sunrise, sunset, moonrise, and moon-set. The phases of the moon are clear depictions in their heads so that later when they cover the math of orbits in school, it settles into their neurons quite easily. They understand life science as they watch the development of animals constantly. Growing plants day in and day out translates a huge amount of information.

When an activity is done only twice, there is a prayer that it will be remembered. When it is performed repeatedly, dendrites have a great grip on each other. When it is covered only once, diligently or not, it's gone.

In my class, we take notice of the moon phase every day. We check the visibility of planets every day. We do weather station, etc. **every day.**

It stands to reason that if it is November, the material from September needs to be dragged out in a meaningful way. When I was a middle school math teacher in the 70s, homework was five different problems from five different weeks. If you don't use it, you lose it. In my science class, the last fifteen minutes of the period are learning centers. Some activities are from topics a month ago, some are current, and some are coming soon in the future. It allows kids to have a feeling of autonomy to select their activities. It keeps the ball in the air. You can't learn and remember "volume displacement method" in one lab. Kids choose that particular learning center over and over. Moon phases and mechanical energy can't be taught in a day or two and that's exactly what a good science textbook would have a teacher do if they are following the "script." I have a designated student record or draw the moon phase every day for the whole class to see. Likewise, a learning center for mechanical energy is set up *long before* that chapter is read in the text. A learning center for solar energy will linger long after we take the test on energy. Seeing things that are coming soon piques interest and lays a good foundation. Systems-learning is an easy way to keep the ball in the air naturally.

By the way, do you remember how to find the volume of an irregular object? Do you even remember how to do quadratic equations? Keep the ball in the air.

Leaf Litter

Except when there is half a foot of snow on the ground, one of the learning centers in my classroom is the "leaf litter station." In every class, there are a few die-hard regulars who visit it. They coax others to join them. My neighbors probably wonder what I'm doing with the garden glove before I get in the car in the morning. The clear hefty bag comes out and I plunge my hand into the edges of the driveway or right into the garden if it's spring. Three or four heaping handfuls of delicious leaf litter go into the bag and the bag goes into the trunk. "Please forgive me, little creatures . . ." At school, the bag gets dumped into a large, white gardening pan. At learning center time, I have to plead with my regulars to sometimes let others explore this fecund, busy microcosm. There is no other plainer, easier, unpretentious, fabulous way to see a perfect little ecosystem. The living things don't escape because they need the leaves. Some students write about the actions of the life they see, some write about the food chains they see in real time, and some students get the field guides out and identify the animals, plants, kingdoms, phyla, classes, and/or species. When they're finished, the students know they must spray the pan with three or four squirts of water and gently lay the clear bag on top for the next class. They also know that the bag goes back outside and new leaf litter arrives the next day.

Let Them Beg for Fractions

Some of my fifth grade students look a little unruly sometimes; they're just talkative. Lectures are prohibitive. Instead, I set up the whole room like that corny phrase, "learning centers" worm bins, beetle containers, physics experiments. Action research centers all need people to tend to them. Ongoing art centers, books that need to be read, games to be played all plead for the extraction of information.

Make every day a workshop day, keep putting new stuff out for exploration. Finally someone will say, "When are we going to learn to do fractions?" HOLD OUT. "Hmm, I don't know if you're ready." Let them beg. When you do give in, make it dependent on their own motivation. "See me if you think you're really ready."

Let them assign their own homework. "What do you think you should do for homework? Do you think you should work on nouns and pronouns? Long division? When do you want to start fractions? Just curious."

Memorize That Poem

I just read a beautiful essay in the *NY Times* Sunday Review (August 27, 2017) about memorizing poems. At Sprout House, we had a night (once or twice a year) where we invited parents for "dessert and poetry." This would be for the fourth to sixth graders. We made delicious, homemade desserts like crepes where parents usually helped. The children would recite or read their chosen poem by a famous poet. Yes, I pre-selected and they chose. If they felt like reading, they read but many just recited while we ate dessert. The Times essay by Molly Worthen discusses the fact that memorization has been disdained for a few decades. The current edicts involve inquiry, problem solving, self-made poems, and fact-based self-expression. But when you remember a poem by a great person, (make sure) you take a part of that person's essential brilliance and hold that silhouette up to your own young life. It's like thinking about someone you have a crush on . . . this is them and this is me. Worthen's essay presumes that memorization is painful. I take exception to that idea. When you simply read it once or twice a day, you will eventually know it by heart. That's not a chore. You will feel the endorphins when you summon it up years later.

Metric

It almost feels like a conspiracy when something so dumb as mixing two systems of measurement in the brains of young kids and then expecting them to keep it straight does not dawn on anyone as a problem. It's NOT like being bilingual because two clear cultures and worlds are usually more or less evident. Bilingualism doesn't require precise calculation or multi-step procedures. My sixth graders even look at me suspiciously when I try to explain (after they've read it one or two times) that weight and mass are different. Then the curriculum piles on pounds, grams, kilograms, milligrams, liters, and more. We make looking at food containers a homework assignment. Then we augment that with lots of other activities. Then they get it! But then forget it on the big test. Too much confusion. American kids have a bona fide handicap.

Migration of Monarchs

I have been raising monarch butterflies in my home and classroom for many years, based on the research which concludes that the only migratory butterfly in North America needs a little help. We find a patch of common milkweed, look at the undersides of leaves, and scan for little football-shaped yellow eggs. I don't remember how I learned to do it but I've been reinforced by my knowledgeable friends and co-workers and of course the Monarch Teacher Network. We have containers and rearing cages and then the waiting, and then that transformative release. That is transformative for the human. If you release a monarch in mid to late September with a student, you will never forget each other (or the butterfly). You are bonded in an epiphany of space-time. This ritual comes with the knowledge that this particular monarch must live hundreds of times longer than its sisters and brothers born in June who only live about two weeks. The awe and the worry changes every human who tries to help in the right way. I tell the children that just telling someone who is "weeding" out milkweed how important that plant is, is enough.

My students tend to live and breathe monarchs.

Somewhere else in North America, children have the luck of living in a valley in Mexico where millions of monarchs "sleep" for the winter. This is a sublime experience; however, as I was reading material by a monarch expert, the Mexican children never get to see the other stages of egg, caterpillar, and chrysalis. We are like the blind men and the elephant. Every step we take is flush with objects and systems and we can only attend to the ones we can relate to. At every turn, reality is a matrix of layers that can be extracted for pleasure or knowledge.

The Monarch Teacher Network travels to these wintering valleys in Mexico and California. I have never gone with them because I would not be able to take a vacation in the middle of January. People return having experienced a rapture and most return to Mexico, on subsequent years and even bring their spouses.

I'm going to go out on a clichéd limb and toss out the notion that these raptures are all around us if we look. I have seen them and so have you.

Addendum: Currently the raising of Monarchs is the subject of study for its ethics considerations and efficacy.

Music Certainly

In the realm of spirituality, in a framework of magic, exists a singular state called music. It takes us far away, tosses us frivolously and returns us better than before. Children and adults thrive and show an indisputable strength in its presence. We flourish in unexpected ways with an abundance of music. Second tier, electronically produced music is almost as good as primary production because it is so powerful. Maxine Green was a Columbia University philosophy professor who maintained that the arts should be the backbone of curriculum rather than the cemented structure of testing.

My Conscience is My Boss

My students are motivated because they are doing primary research of their choosing (given options). Some are studying various aspects of aphid behavior; some are studying moths near a lighted window at night; some are canvassing friends and relatives for certain science opinions, etc. My students are motivated because we invest in a literary experience every day for a little while. We refer to it and discuss it and extend it with other activities. My students are motivated because they master all kinds of skills. My students are motivated because they are informed about current issues. My students are motivated because they appreciate and understand the details of the neighborhood (trees, storm drains, plumbing, water supply, birds, stores, businesses, libraries, parks, etc.) In fact, my students make suggestions about the curriculum for themselves and others. Then just when they are at their intellectual apex, the ten-month mark rolls around and they leave me. That needs to change. But beyond that ridiculous tragedy, when things are going really well, a supervisor can trot in, evaluate the setting, and not understand or like an activity (despite the fact that things are going very well) and demand that a minuscule activity be pulled. This is after a forty-minute observation out of 180 days. The activity in question, which is ten minutes of learning-center time where students choose a random, hands-on activity to practice something old or "taste" something on the upcoming agenda, was on the chopping block. Rather than expel the learning centers, which were an enormous amount of work (enough for twenty plus kids), I contemplated the enormous value and continued the practice four to five days per week.

Defiance could render me lonesome for my job. I see and know that when kids are asking for more work, they have more than a good chance of retaining the material. My conscience will have to be my boss.

Nature

My science supervisor scoffed with a dismissive chuckle when I suggested that life science be taught when the children had the most access to outdoor activities such as September, October, April, May, June, and physical science be taught in the winter. No discussion followed; we moved on to a discussion of "data", but not actually studying any relevant data. The subject, and my comment were ignored like sparrows in a city park.

Why create huge, costly set-ups in labs when you can go outside and experience complex macro and micro systems all performing without any effort to students and teachers. Not contrived ….real ! Balance, then instability, then balance again in a system for all to study in real time. Too many variables, maybe, but real learning. What a concept! Luckily, squirrels can be monitored all year or for an hour to see their physicality, interactions with each other and other species. Their food preferences, their homes, mating and nurturing offspring make easy studies of equilibrium and risks. The insect world and even the world of algae are all there for perfect ongoing dynamic systems of learning. The world is our oyster and corporate curriculum continues to rob it and some science supervisors continue to scoff.

"OBJECTIVES" and Jargon

Writing lesson plan objectives is a new religion. Each objective has three parts: the "behavior," the "condition," and the "measure." Blah, blah, blah.

They are enshrined in the "planbook" and then written on the white board or chalkboard, and even the best of students start weeping because they don't understand them. Sometimes students are required to write them. This takes more than three minutes for the last child to finish. In my case, these children are sixth and seventh graders.

Friday, February 2

Behavior: Analyze the data in bar and line graph form while completing questions based on that data then complete an intake sheet.

Condition: Given a graph with the data on peregrine falcon productivity in NJ in 2012, we all learn to (W.A.L.T.)

Measure: Answer five questions correctly, one of which is in paragraph format in thirty-five minutes.

Now that lesson doesn't sound particularly compelling but the students actually had been viewing nesting adults and eggs, then chicks for weeks and weeks via a webcam so they had a serious interest in this species. We had chosen this species because falcons were in the neighborhood, actually on the building next door, preying on rock pigeons.

The encoded torture session of "objectives" is contrary to every lesson (and format) developed in the past twenty years. Perhaps this is because some of the adults masquerading as teachers are not truly dedicated professionals, and/or that teachers as a group have not won the confidence of the administration or the general public. The reasoning is that this writing requirement will magically turn those folks into effective teachers. But reality is that the good teachers get bogged down laboriously tinkering with the wording and lose time they need to gather and produce materials and plan for the next day or week. The result: the good teachers are frustrated and the less-than-good teachers are more lost than ever. Where does that leave students?

As far as WALT (we-all-learn-to) goes, WALT is about to morph into SWBAT (students-will-be-able-to). In the 1970s, teachers were forbidden to write the word "learn" in an objective because they had no immediate proof of learning. Objectives needed to be stated behaviorally (students will complete three quadratic equations correctly). The jargon fluctuates back and forth, year-to-year or decade to decade in hopes that the jargon will neurologically create great teachers out of mediocre teachers. Again, jargon impedes great teachers and renders mediocre teachers into slush.

Palace in Your Place

"Open your textbook to page 259", not because there is something that relates to the trees outside our classroom window or the weather we are experiencing, or because it shows a similar mountain range as ours, or there is an explanation of the alternative energy we are using in our school, or because it explains the bedrock we have, or because there is a description of the bird migration that takes place over our community, but because we just finished page 258!" Yawn, yawn, and stagnation.

"Place-Based Education" should have been a buzz phrase, but alas, nobody can make money on it. Dr. David Sobel and the Orion Society developed the phrase and concept. It's the study of the spider on the corner wall, or the leaf litter packed down under the shrub outside, or the wildflower (weed) growing out of the sidewalk. Make your bedrock samples into household words. Harvest a few slugs and snails and respect them. Spend time in October, after you've gotten to know your students, with a bag of leaf litter. Clumped in wet, smelly, rotting layers on any urban sidewalk, volumes of life can be tossed into a garbage bag and brought up to the classroom. Get as close as you can to this dense marvel, smell the smells, and listen to tiny little rustlings. Left out on a white plastic tray or table, the most wonderful, ambitious creatures will reveal themselves in a few minutes. Better yet, put it in the biggest sieve or colander you can find, with a clean, new, white kitty litter pan underneath. Shine a desk lamp into the sieve with all the leaf litter. The invertebrates will crawl out quicker as they try to escape the heat and light. Be as respectful as you can. Return them outside at the end of day. This honest and intimate microcosm of life, complex yet simple, is one vital end of a food web and as such and for many reasons will captivate many students. A platform to study any number of things, it can be with or without academic strings attached. This kind of learning is tireless luxury, and triggers lifelong propensities for wanting more.

A corollary to Place Based Ed is the way I have tried to teach science. Instead of following the textbook page by page, chapter by chapter, we study the common materials in our lives (water, peroxide, seltzer, soap, bleach, baking soda, lemon juice, salt, sugar, honey, red cabbage, green cabbage, acorns, sunblock, milk, oil, vinegar, flour, wax, plastics, etc.).

The idea is to perform a variety of tests on each. These are very simple tests but with good scientific method. Does it evaporate? Does it dissolve? Does it freeze? Does it melt? At what temperature? Does stirring speed up the process? What elements are in it? What compounds? Ask all the essential questions about your everyday substances. Findings are recorded carefully. Graphs are designed when applicable. Too often we disrespect the fact that most textbook experiments are performed on materials students don't have experience with. They sometimes take concepts out of thin air, and disregard the need to focus on half steps up from where a student is cognitively. We also ignore the fact that in our technologically layered post-modern world, some students don't know much about simple basic substances and systems around us.

STOP WHAT YOU ARE DOING. Monarch butterflies are visiting the school yard, so drop what you are doing and focus on this instead. This is a spectacular migration phenomenon. Shame on you if you don't have a general understanding of it! Applaud yourself if you don't know something about what's happening and you admit it, then find out what you can, with or without the students. Your call.

A peregrine falcon is dive-bombing pigeons from the building next door.

A new water main is being installed in the street outside the school. Do the kids understand infrastructure ?

A lunar eclipse will occur tonight. Provide background and encourage (not require) all to view it. Call the education department of your main newspaper. See if they will deliver enough papers for each kid in your class for that special day. At the time of this writing, newspapers are in tenuous fiscal condition, and publishers are looking for any and every promotional angle. My paper had a newspaper in education program that promoted readership to youth. Sometimes they have grant money for a temporary or permanent delivery. It might just be a few days a week.

A small meteorite hit the moon, leaving a ten-foot diameter crater. (*True Story*, November 2005)

Field trips (see separate essay) Consider nearby trips. Study what is under your feet, over your head, and next to you. Kids should understand their chunk of the earth, their bio-region. If they truly understand their own natural, culturally constructed, and commercially constructed habitat, they will be more prone to being curious about others and have more brain connection-frameworks for other applications. A trip is a moment. Capture the moment.

PLACE-BASED RESEARCH

Ask children to study a behavior (Action Research) in the community. How many times in a week did you hear someone say something positive about a sibling? Record data. How much trash do you pick up every day in one square meter of sidewalk? Record the data. How many kids eat the fruit on their lunch tray?

PLACE-based physical science: Spray a mild perfume by the classroom radiator and record the direction of how it floats around the room to get a sense of the convection current. Do it in the winter when the heat is on. Compare it to the summer when the windows are open and days when the windows are closed and no heat is on. Draw diagrams with arrows.

DINOSAURS! Which dinosaurs walked on the ground in *your* neighborhood? Those should be the names that roll off kid's tongues. Facility with information about those animals will make your neighborhood come alive into an intellectual empire. Find them in your local museums, look on-line, and contact the geology department at your state university.

Jerry Schierloh, instructor at School of Conservation in Stokes State Forest developed the Ecolological Address form. Each student is given the form to fill in their own bedrock, native mammals, native wildflowers, annual precipitation, growing season, and eighty other items that every human should take responsibility of knowing. Bravo, Jerry and Bravo, David. Mr. Schierloh and Mr. Sobel deserve a huge amount of credit for promoting the emergent curriculum in what is known as Place Based Education.

Repeat After Me….Science Is….

Repeat after me, science is great….science is great….science is great ….science is ….

I was visiting my aunt and uncle in Northern Florida over spring break. Before I got ready to go to the airport to come home to NJ, I asked them if I could take some of their gigantic "pine" cones in their back yard from their Loblolly tree. They said, "Of course." Being about ten inches long, only three would fit in a plastic grocery-store bag. I was greedy and took two store bags for a total of six. After I returned my rental car, I found out that bad weather in New Jersey was going to prevent my flight from leaving. I sat on the floor, leaning up against the wall and slept for six hours clutching my backpack and the six loosely bagged "pine cones."

When the flight eventually took off, my backpack went into the upper storage area and the two recycled bags with giant "pine" cones were either on my lap or at my feet, intermittently, for the actual flight.

The next day, I brought them to class and made them into a learning center with field guides. The students who chose this activity were to research the cones and determine the species of tree. This activity was chosen in all five of my first classes and it turned out to be easy peasy because of the size of cones. Many students handled the "pine" cones. In the sixth class (my last for the day), a group was doing the activity on a desk, when a student said loudly in an inflected, surprised voice, "Ms. White, something jumped out of the cone!" I looked down, and a scorpion hurried across the floor. Keep in mind that one of my students had given me the nickname, Ghostbuster, due to my technique of catching many flying things when they finally alight in classroom, as I always keep windows wide open. My act consists of calmly putting a plastic deli container over the creature, then slide a slick cardboard piece of junk mail under it, flip it holding the cardboard securely and carry it to the window and release it without ado. (Mr. White taught it to me.) This time, however, after starting the Ghostbuster routine, I instructed a student to hand me a rectangle Chinese-food container and lid. We popped the scorpion into the new container and got that lid on fast. I punched teeny holes in it. The next day, I brought a juicy, decomposing local pine cone full of mud and soil and organisms, and, with the help of a student, popped it into the container to supply the scorpion with some food and a habitat. Every few days, we changed out the pinecone. We realized it wasn't a big eater, so we did it less frequently, maybe every ten days. The end of June rolled around and the last few days of school being frantic, the Chinese-food container got dumped in a box and stored in the closet by a student helping me to pack. Bad teacher. I never even remembered it. Fast forward to the look on my face in September when I unpacked the Chinese-food container. Little Scorpy was alive and well, sparking research ideas galore. Love that science.

Rigor and Cooking

It's fall of 2013. My school district wants to see RIGOR in our lessons. I design a world without "fill in the blanks." My students, instead, are required to fashion concepts in paragraph format. I keep it simple, one concept at a time. They need the practice because many have great difficulty with sentences, spelling, and summarizing. It's so tough, that 10 percent don't even try. I have enough issues teaching science that I can't take on all issues of language arts, so we just plod along. Then the edict comes that students can't get a grade less than 50 percent. Sounds compassionate, but it's not. The student that tried and got half the work right gets the same grade as the one that didn't bother. So now we cook the books while demanding rigor at the same time.

Spatial

My sixth grade science students have great difficulties with spatial learning. This includes things like:

- the solar system is in the Milky Way galaxy

- Earth's continents are on tectonic plates

- the deeper the fossil, the older the organism

- the inner core of Earth is solid because the three other layers are pressing in

- a cold front hits a warm front in a different way than a warm front hits a cold front (even though my students understand the nature of warm molecules and cold molecules and that warm air rises and cold air sinks)

- diagrams of animals adapting to different conditions with branching changes/results

- and above all: the northern hemisphere pictured with Arctic Ocean in the middle of the "circle."

To take a step back, I give them the assignment of drawing a map of the classroom. What I get back are the most beautiful Picassos. Gorgeous renderings of every detail you could imagine: the manual pencil sharpener, the flag, the plants, the balance scale, the microscopes, arrays for desks and the phases of the moon. But the door and windows are not just in the wrong place; they're twisted and flipped.

It's a screaming reminder that nothing is logical in this for-profit fun-house we call public education. The kids are so mixed up by every new innovation that is shoved toward certain schools. No concept is built on the previous foundation. It's all a frantic new workshop or buzzword to attend to and then implement. It's frequently a new technology to flaunt.

Yes, the result is extraordinarily interesting art ….but at great academic expense.

Spirit Quest

A really good field trip where the natural phenomena are magical, can serve as a mini spirit quest, which is absent in our culture. This is a place where the building of your first campfire or feeling your first success at flint knapping brings on some very quiet rapture.

In my childhood, the flood of euphoria from climbing to the top of a very tall tree, then the bonus of a *view* expanded my desire to soak up all this world could show me. Walking into the main hall of United Nations and seeing the General Assembly in session was, to say the least, *mind blowing.*

One of my favorite activities for my students is sitting in a place for three to fifteen minutes with little movement and no sound. The natural world emerges and moves closer and closer. Centipedes, chipmunks, and birds reenact a Disney movie as they "forget" that you are even present.

People who miss profound formative experiences are always searching and sometimes in the wrong places.

Storytime and the Dichotomy of Racism

The teachers, who taught with me at Sprout House, ingrained in me a deeper reverence for something I already respected greatly. Storytime became an almost divine part of the day. Not just in the nursery school, but in the elementary school. Everyone stops what they're doing to share in a tale. There's an aura in the room as the teacher subtly dramatizes with voice inflections only. Its duration depends on the story, the children's ages, and the day's activities, but it is a downright spiritual experience. Everyone is in it together. Some students just listen. Some students draw (usually related to the story) and some students take their Ziploc bag of clay or play dough and create aspects of the story. Great discussions usually follow the passages.

Occasionally, if I have chosen a classic from my childhood or even one a mere twenty years old, I have been shocked into the practice of the dreaded impromptu "revisionism." Beloved stories can be so riddled with unacceptable citations. How can authors from another time be so strongly supportive of humanity and sensitive to injustice and use such racist language? My cherished *A Stranger at Green Knowe, Dickon Among the Lenapes,* and *Little House on the Prairie*, only name a few. It breaks my heart to toss such well-meaning works of art. It constitutes evidence that racism is ingrained, unconscious and systemic.

Stream Studies

The best field trip there is for humans on a hot day is a stream study. With modifications, any age will be interested and most will try every activity offered. Simple gear (dip nets for each child, a few plastic jars, pH paper optional, old sneakers, change of clothes or bathing suit, drinking water, small towel) is needed with the teacher bringing along a few extras. The first requirement is safety. The teacher must scope out a section of a healthy, non-muddy stream for considerations such as, slipperiness, ease of slope, and depth of water (knee high to the children). Establish rules while still in the classroom such as, "when you hear the whistle freeze immediately, and listen for directions." Water flow can be noisy, so practice. Be gentle with animals …. very, very gentle.

When the spot is reached, make sure all belongings are carefully deposited in logical areas and everyone has a buddy. Give each child a dip net with a number. Fill the jars with stream water and tell the students where each is located.

As a group, take the pH (potential of hydrogen) and compare it to drinking water. No lectures; wait until you return to the classroom, just remember the results.

If kids are unfamiliar with the outdoors, just let them enjoy the physics of walking or sitting in the stream. Soon they will see a water strider or a crayfish and the rejoicing will begin. They will build pools or dams with cobbles, watch their "catch" in a plastic jar, share ideas with each other and probably try to swim. The habitat that is so different from living in your house, will provide a matrix/new puzzle for understanding the pieces as they organically absorb the information around them.

Many books and websites can explain to nonscience teachers wonderful activities for a stream setting. But this is not necessary at all. The idea is to let them construct their own knowledge **without** too many lectures. They are building logical mental structures by themselves (according to Jean Piaget) with which to build facts. These self-directed connecting nuggets will be remembered.

Safety is paramount….choose good chaperones.

Don't leave animals in the jar for more than nine minutes, even in the shade.

Count heads, count heads, count heads.

If you can't find a clear, clean stream, that's a lesson in itself.

Subject-Verb

How hard is it to make up relevant worksheets for your students? Why aren't students' own journals their "reading materials?"

Underline the subject once. Underline the verb twice.

1. On the playground, before school, Belle Terre Academy has a secret way to know the air temperature.

2. The American sycamore tree still has a few leaves left and it is the end of November.

3. Our class will put together another songbook.

4. On the Wednesday before Thanksgiving, we ate a healthful snack.

5. For cancer prevention, the snack included red cabbage.

6. For a Thanksgiving food, the snack included cranberries.

1. New Jersey is the cranberry capital of the world.

2. We will see if the redworms mix up the bran flakes.

3. Instead of monarchs, we are now seeing many birds of prey.

4. We did not know it, but we brought a living barnacle back to school.

5. The students caught grass shrimp with nets at the Hackensack Meadowlands.

6. The museum at the Hackensack Meadowlands had bigger-than-life examples of the habitat and the wildlife.

7. Why are we taking Cycle Tests?

Synthesis Paper

Adams State College and the American Museum of Natural History

Spiders in the Field

Summer 2005

When I first became aware of a course devoted entirely to the subject of spiders, I saw perfect alignment with the environmental education objectives I was seeking in terms of my urban, middle school students. At age fifty-one,

I challenged myself to move from a suburban setting to a city school district. I am an environmental educator by experience, not by certification. I have managed and led adventure camps, stream studies, herptile studies, and vernal pool studies for the NJ Department of Environmental Protection (DEP) and local wildlife centers. Besides the two class-time field trips and afterschool field trips, I still wanted more for my students, whose families, for whatever reasons, don't end up in very many natural settings on the weekends. In the course description, it stated, "No matter where you are, you are always only ten feet from a spider," and this made sense to me for environmental education in the city. I really felt that I would like to turn at least some of my students into budding arachnologists.

As a middle school science teacher, I would, from time to time, sit down with a spider field guide, but never advance very far in my understanding. I have been frustrated learning the spiders of my area, especially so because I have made many attempts. The mystery of not being able to crack the spider code and the fact that there are spiders everywhere for urban students are the two reasons I took this course. The following discussion explains how the outcomes even exceeded those expectations.

Last summer (2004), I was lucky enough to get a grant to work with a researcher out of state, (on a different subject) and that was a wonderful adventure. This summer (2005) was going to be a letdown compared to that stimulating science experience. Because of some moderately serious health issues and related treatments I had no choice but to stay home and take an online class. The class unfolded in a remarkable way. My house, yard, and adjacent County Park became a sustaining, logical, and compelling laboratory inquest. Every morning, I inspected every inch of my yard, and found the most competent engineering in the most intriguing places. I learned how even a thirty-minute change in light can camouflage a web. I saw things that, of course, were always there but were now accessible to my brain, like thirty-five babies riding on the back of the mother, four-foot webs taken down every night and rebuilt the next day, very complicated courtship and sexual behavior, stunning aerial gymnastics, and sublime mastery of geometric lodgings. I was content to be home and began to enjoy the solitude and thoroughness of my immersion. One outcome was gaining greater skill in journaling. I have always been "big" on journals, but I expanded my skills to include better scientific protocol, details, and scientific sketching. I was forced to improve my digital photography skills and the incorporation of them into reports. The journal and the photography became part of the lab experience as well. The lab also included the examination of specimens with lenses and microscope, and the very careful cataloguing, labeling, and correlation with the journal. I spent lots of time absolutely "losing myself" in many activities, an example of which was sketching the size and configuration and arrangement of six or eight eyes.

Through the labs and required diagramming, morphology and anatomy were systematically being understood. In addition, learning spider classification went well, as I expected. I also cleared up another problem: many older books have terms that have been dropped or changed, especially in species classification. So it wasn't me after all.

As far as skills and teaching methods, for this project, they were counterpoint. I came away with a really rich and full bag of tricks, which will captivate my students. My students, especially because they are surrounded by so much concrete, want as much "hands-on" environmental education as possible. There were six pieces of lab equipment for spider collection, and five of them were made from items found in a supermarket or hardware store. The items themselves could be student-made in the lab! All five pieces of equipment were safe to construct and handle. This was an outcome I did not expect, so it was a bonus. The sixth item, the aspirator, (containment with suction) could be made at home for perhaps a science fair project. The grand culminating pinnacle is of course that spiders are everywhere, under radiators, in windowsills, under desks, in courtyards, and schoolyards.

The attached project is an in-depth unit of lesson plans developed from the course "In the Field with Spiders." The actual lab work that we did as graduate students, observing, collecting and sketching, will be done without any amendments with my seventh graders. The recording of behavior will have somewhat simpler requirements as you will read. However, I will refer to the species by the Linnaean classification as well as the common name, because we have already established that routine in my classes. In terms of equipment, the "aspirator" will only be demonstrated for health reasons, but with encouragement to make one at home. All other collecting equipment will be used.

As far as outcomes with respect to information, the students in my classes enjoy having a working knowledge of science topics that are accessible, such as using the meteorology instruments. They manipulate the instruments, record the data, discuss it, share it with other communities, and therefore don't even realize the great facility they have with all the facts, terminology, and applications. I think the same will be true with the spider collection process. They will want to succeed in collecting, identifying, and labeling for our lab/ museum. Personally, I had the same experience as I took the course. I ended up knowing many new species easily identifiable and the framework to figure out new ones. Spider anatomy, functions, and behavior are now comprehensible due to the process of journaling and the slow and steady introduction and use of the dichotomous key.

As you read the attached project, you will see that the culminating activity is to create a binder-size, local spider field guide, by my science club students. I have already started it to stimulate some excitement. Another interesting outcome is that in the past two weeks, it has occurred to me that we can do this for all kinds of natural phenomenon, such as roadside "wildflowers," urban birds, etc.

Technology Integration May 9, 2010

According to the Glencoe textbook, technology is the practical use of science, or applied science. In my classroom, we use various forms of technology on a routine basis, frequently referring back to previous tools and technological skills. We use all of the following, sometimes daily: binoculars, telescopes, spectroscopes, photovoltaic cells, hygrometer, home-made barometer, sundial, simple machines, iPad vs. book assessment, keystone arch engineering, sustainability websites for baseline numbers of species, webcams, spray bottles, etc.

- Webcams: Every day we check on "our" peregrine falcon chicks and "our" bald eagle chicks <u>live.</u> We keep it on in the background so that when an egg hatches or a parent brings prey, the students have a complete organic grasp of the animal and they internalize the information.

- Research: Daily science current events

- Earth Day Bio Blitz: Students are in the process of researching local species, soil, and mineral samples

- PBwiki After researching an endangered animal in its ecosystem to understand sustainability, students posted their research on the class website. This was a work in progress.

- Photostory : Students create a visual presentation of their work. Students researched seven questions, found appropriate images, and summarized the cogent concepts for a photostory movie that will be finished in a few weeks. They used microphones for narration and developed a critical eye for results that would be aesthetic and factual. Even the students who are finished continue to tweak the movie and the wiki to improve it.

- Best technology integration: In our un-air-conditioned school building, students ask to use my spray bottle with cold water on their faces, when they can't take the heat anymore.

The Classroom as a Living Workshop

I keep shamelessly boasting that no two years have ever been alike in this 40 plus years career. But it's true. Would it appeal to you if the meteorologists gave the same weather report every day, every year? It's as silly as that if you think about it. Why would we want children to be in four walls with stagnant information? The same classroom as the children the year before and the year before that. Brand new textbooks contain three year old information the moment the first child cracks open the brand new volume. Anyone who does not feel smothered by that notion is brainwashed by an entrenched system.

The absurdity of ignoring current events in middle school social studies is not apparent in many school systems. There are twenty-first century science books that claim that all life depends on the sun for energy. How tough is that mistake? Although arguable, chemosynthesis from the ocean vents could be the driving force of an entire fifth grade curriculum to include life in outer space. That's why students complain that school is so b-word.*   It's not organic enough; in fact, it's quite dead. Do all middle school students wait with bated breath for what and who wins all the Nobel prizes?

Classrooms need to be living, breathing, organic systems. Let's throw out the baby and definitely the dismal, tired, vexing bath water. As John Taylor Gatto* reminded us emphatically that we should not continue to honor the Prussian military model as a school model. We're not good listeners.

* boring

*Dumbing Us Down by John Taylor Gatto

The Flipped Classroom Ha, Ha, Ha

Another trendy workshop skill that good teachers have used forever, and forever means before technology, is the "flipped classroom." "Go home and draw this diagram on page 145 and tomorrow we will discuss it, and then we will do an activity or lab in the classroom tomorrow." This and other similar activities have been used for a hook, for a long time. It's positively laughable that someone thinks they invented running water. The classroom is the place for the discussion and the *activity,* and always has been for good teachers, end of story. The trick is to make that homework something that is not a snoozefest and something they will actually do, such as sketching something.

In case you are unfamiliar with the phrase "flipped classroom," it refers to the new obsession to send students home to watch some sort of video to prepare them for the activity the following day. It shortens the time for lecture and gives them a so-called quieter place to digest material at their own pace. It's a great technique but it's not the Ten Commandments.

It's just a part of good teaching. One classroom in a school just north of Detroit had great success with it. C+ was the lowest average in the class. The principal then forced it on the whole school. So again, whatever was going on in other classrooms that might have been tailored to those individuals was disrespected, instead of just suggesting or encouraging the idea.

The Ice Cracks

Two grandchildren, 8 and 2 years old are with me often. We're out for a lovely winter walk in the woods, city, driveway, park, or gutter. If there's a stick and ice to break and experiment with, maybe a little puddle…, we are understatedly euphoric. They don't even ***need*** to look at someone else for a smile connection, they're just smiling to themselves. They pick up a piece of ice, break the ice, hold it up to the sun, look at the bubbles, etc. These folks are solid, liquid, gas experts because they are going to bash and thrash the material to joyful oblivion. Don't forget the sounds. How many cracking sounds are possible? Which shapes slide the farthest? Add mud…now we're really communing with the definition of play. How long will this last? I am a little frozen in many ways, but they will continue until the second set of boots and mittens are wet and the onset of hypothermia. Good potential researchers for Enceladus, the moon of Saturn.

Three Goals (Choose)

Every teacher needs to contemplate their goals, forcing brevity and conviction. Brainstorm a long list at first, then reflect and weed out. Be prepared to support your choices. Here is **my** road to academic prosperity for my students.

Happiness

Self-motivation

Earth Literacy

1. Happiness: Some people live without it. Unhappiness is a tough trip given that when additional disappointments pile up, the bad bulge pushes onto other things. Consequently, it's a firm mandate that classroom culture needs to be predominantly bubbly with scholarly energy. Students' positive voices plow through classroom consciousness. "Let's try this kind of shelter for our caterpillar!" " Let's try watering with a spray bottle!" "Can we read this next?" "I saw the same bird that was in the poem!" This, of course, is without artificial incentives, just joyful understanding. Some teachers can make kids happy with candy. They should, respectfully, learn how to teach. Their hearts are in the right place.

2. Self-Motivation: When a student decides she likes a certain author, fiction genre, or nonfiction subject, and begs for more, that child is educated. When students ask so many higher-order questions (horizontal curriculum) that it's hard to proceed with the vertical curriculum, go to the library or internet and let them loose for a little while. Here is an example. We were methodically detailing the origin of the Solar System. Part of it included, "a shock wave from a distance, hit the cloud of gas and dust, and it started to rotate." The questions I got were: 1. A shock wave from where? In galaxy or out of galaxy? 2. Was the cloud a nebula or a nova? 3. Was the cloud moving at all before it got hit?

   In a small class with behavior-challenged kids, I spent a week in September doing graphic art 8 out of 8 periods a day for a week to calm them down and wipe out the behavior. Although a great calm prevailed, even with the students who claimed, "I can't draw!" by the following Tuesday, two boys came to me and said, "When are we going to do fractions?"

   I said, "Not yet." I got a funny look but no argument. By Friday, they were begging for fractions. Eureka!

3. Earth Literacy: Mother Earth is the giver of all givers. She gives. We take. It's the only thing that matters. We derive pleasure from its beauty, comfort from its fertile offerings, and stimulation from its

magnetic and engrossing opportunities. Students naturally plumb its gifts knowledgeably. Respect for the latest calamities of climate change preoccupy young people, as it should.

The contemplative exercise of clarifying three personal teaching goals will dredge up lots of important conclusions for any teacher, in any subject, in any age group.

Too Busy REPRESENTING Things (the prostitution of literacy)

Walk into 75 percent of all classrooms in America and you will not see evidence of KNOWLEDGE but evidence of the representation of knowledge. We are SO obsessed with the skill of coding and decoding that we sometimes forget the information itself. Walls are plastered with charts on how to conjugate verbs, change decimals to percentages, define what a paragraph is, decipher a verb from a noun, that there isn't a shred of what it is you are using those codes for. A great number of classrooms have no seeds/plants, no circuits, no bridges, no art materials, no percussion instruments, but plenty of schlocky reading rather than great literature for the most part.

It's no wonder kids space out. That's not what kids relate to. They want to do things.

Totality and the Awesomeness of Earth Math

I have never been able to make a pilgrimage to Mexico to see the monarch butterflies clustered in winter in the Oyamel trees, but I did see thousands clustered in seaside goldenrod at Sandy Hook, NJ. Your heart remains calm but your nervous system perks up in a good way and you look at the person next to you with a relaxed, ridiculous grin that just won't stop. Sounds like a contradiction, but it isn't. Of course the same thing happened for my first horseshoe crab/red knot migration and the Garter snake emergence day at Lord Stirling Park in Spring. These miraculous events remind you how the Bible tells humans that nature moves your spiritual side as it smothers with a rapture. My multi-age Sprout House class went on an overnight trip to Cape May (my first time in the early '90s) in time with the full moon in May. The word "spectacle" is not an exaggeration. Each child had chosen a shorebird to track (red knot, sanderling, ruddy turnstone, etc.). They learned how scientists count large numbers . . . and why. Boy, did they learn how scientists count large numbers! They mapped the exact migration route from **northern** North America to **southern** South America for their particular species, studied habitats, reproduction, food web, etc. They were experts. Thousands upon thousands of horseshoe crabs and the individual shorebirds transformed "wow" into intellectual bliss. Similarly, I was walking with my class in Lord Stirling Park on a sunny day the third week in March in the '90s again. We had seen lots of birds and mammals and were heading back to the Environmental Center on an official path. I spied a garter snake to the left and said to the student at the front of the line, "Look, Andrew, there's a sleepy garter." Andrew faced forward. I repeated it. He still looked forward. I raised my voice for the third repetition and he said, "*I **am** looking at the garter snake.*" I focused my eyes a little more to gain on camouflage and realized there were hundreds, if not thousands of garters rolling around in balls in a romantic stupor. We stood still because they actually rolled over some of our feet in a blanket-like movement and rolled on. Think about how bonded the humans now were to each other with a giddy, euphoric chill. Back at the building, the environmentalists said warmly but matter-of-factly, "Oh yeah, that's the emergence." Again, the counting lesson.

The total eclipse in 2017 had so much math going on that I had to chill from the math on and off. The showstopper for me is the utter, ultimate coincidence of the sun being 400 times bigger than the moon, and coincidentally, the moon being 1/400th of the distance making them a perfect fit in shadow, at least for now. Any good book on the subject will offer it. My childlike brain prefers to fixate on the coincidence.

Tutoring and Half Steps

Now that I am tutoring, in my little retirement realm, I realize that "one-on-one" allows a relaxed world. Whatever words of wisdom I had for a class of twenty, they were just lightning type lucky gems in a fuzzy, often chaotic scene. As I speak to the students I now tutor, I wish I could have had the luxury of EXPLAINING the way I can now. When kids say, "I can't do this" or "I'm not good at this," the teacher's response should always be the following: "That means you are missing a step or a half step. You just need to isolate the part you don't understand and go back until you hit the step or half step that you <u>do</u> understand. Come after school, or research it yourself."

I didn't say this nearly enough, I realize now. Because really, since that's all tutoring is about, I regret that this little bit of strengthening didn't happen more often in my classroom.

Vertical Curriculum and Horizontal Curriculum

The Vertical Curriculum is one in which **representational/symbolic skills** (or any other lockstep progression of skills) are mastered with a few practice experiences and then the individual moves on up the "ladder" to the next representational/symbolic skill.

Examples

"MATH"	"LANGUAGE ARTS"
One-to-one Correspondence	Letter recognition
Matching	Letter-sound recognition
Sequencing	Initial consonants
Sets	Ending consonants
Counting	Consonant blends
Adding	Consonant digraphs
Subtracting	Short vowels
Tens	Long vowels with silent "e"
Hundreds	Long vowel sounds with two vowels
Thousands	Combinations
Arrays	Word endings
2-D shapes	Plurals
Fraction identification	Vowels tied to "r"
Multiplication	Double consonants

Measuring inches, feet, yards	"igh" "ould" "ough"
Calendar calculations	Silent letters
Elapsed time, etc.	"ie" vs. "ei," etc.

(The list above goes beyond a typical five-year-old curriculum and is meant only to illustrate Vertical Curriculum).

Five-year-olds might be able to remember a few sight words and a few relevant letters and numbers, and some may be able to phonetically decipher the straight lines and curved lines into meaning and quantities. Until they are overloaded, they might even find it challenging and interesting.

With any skill set, however, there are many "horizontal" opportunities.

The Horizontal Curriculum looks sideways in every direction to think about many perspectives on the *same* level *before* moving on to more complicated representational/symbolic skills.

HORIZONTAL : Examples for Early Childhood:

Wind, water, precipitation, clouds, lightning, squirrels, rabbits, deer, birds, amphibians, turtles, spiders, insects, trees, shrubs, native plants, native flowers, fungi, ferns, seeds, vegetables, fruits, soil, rocks, bedrock, sand, streams, solids, liquids, decomposition, forces, energy, sound, light, heat, cold, bubbles, paper, simple machines, hammers, drills, balls, spectrums, magnets, metals, shadows, floating, sinking, planting, climbing, stores, police, firefighters, plumbers, electricians, buildings, bridges, tunnels, cars, planes, helicopters, bikes, trikes, seasons, the daytime moon and last but not least, native people.

In other words: studying the world and evidence.

(*Literary Experiences and the Arts go without saying apart or embedded in both realms.)

There is a never-ending list of things to study at one's own developmental level (horizontal) rather than "advancing" up the vertical ladder before that child is "asking" to do so. You can not run out of horizontal ideas. The Vertical Curriculum is often relied upon by teachers to impress, for parental approval, and to elicit recognition with easy so-called gains. The Horizontal

Curriculum, which almost always overlaps the emergent curriculum, requires diligence, imagination, and creativity on the part of the teacher. Employing the Vertical Curriculum is more expedient, often ignoring the emergent curriculum. However, *individualizing* the vertical Curriculum (V.C.) honors the child's abilities but it is rarely employed with less than a group of children.

When a child is not ready for a new representational/symbolic skill, there is always exhaustive science and social studies to ponder, savor, enjoy, and *retain.* Some would also argue that the unconscious malaise that sets in when students are not prime candidates for a given vertical skill, manifests itself in behavior issues.

When 15 to 20 percent of the population is diagnosed with "reading problem" and disability labels, there's good reason to look toward the confusion of straight lines and curved lines not having been rooted in systemic meaning.

Both the H.C. and V.C. are needed in the education of every child. Finessing the landscape is the art of teaching. The H.C. should be geared to the student's own setting for genuine, systemic, immersive learning. The V.C. should be more individualized, to avoid superficial, achievement-oriented, and reductionist school experiences. Boasting, even understated boasting, comes at a price.

H.C. is about systems. V.C. is about steps. When the V.C. is not abused for pretension, both are wonderful ways of approaching a content-rich program. The Horizontal Curriculum is the compelling underpinning for humans to **want** to symbolically represent something. Without a strong knowledge base, symbols are wobbly, shallow, and amusingly unnecessary. They therefore present as a pretentious hazard for too many children when developmental levels don't correlate.

What Would an Organic Classroom Do for All of Us?

It might look a little like an interactive museum, a lot like a workshop, a lot like a lab, a little like a library, and a little like home. Instead of looking like preparation for something or even preparation for adulthood, it should look like an important and well-thought-out way for kids to spend their day. If not, it's a sobering waste of childhood.

Kids may not consciously realize their childhoods have been squandered by adults. Adults who profit from products and materials that don't uplift, expand, or inspire, or adults who merely punch in and punch out every day have wasted more than just youthful potential. Unconscious frustration will be manifested one negative way or another, exponentially, kid by kid, which is not productive for them or society.

When to Go Deep and When Not to

A teacher can break all rules as long as they are honest and determined, thorough and mindful of their individual students. Do you want to study the Oak tree outside the classroom window in depth, or do you want to map every tree in the schoolyard, or give them a choice? Every class is different and every year is different. The question is which will provide more relevance and learning pleasure. I have classes where students forgot 89 percent of the science content because there was just too much of it. However if it builds, according to me and all of brain research, where one fact is dependent on another, they will, of course, remember it. Endless names of human anatomy, enzymes, and functions will not be remembered by sixth graders. Less is more. If you only teach the major skeletal bones, they have a chance. Nursing students on the other hand, who will use this info and manipulate the concepts, will remember it. (Sixth grade brains and twenty-year-old brains have the same basic capabilities.)

Another way to look at it is to label it the "horizontal" or "vertical curriculum." Does a student want to learn a lot about one thing, or have the pleasure of laying out and identifying all the objects in a system? One child may absorb the life cycle and habitat needs of a frog and another student may find great rewards in knowing all the frogs of NORTHERN NJ. This concept is prodigiously illuminated by Joanne Hendrick in *The Whole Child*, Pearson, 1988.

It's up to the child and you.

Who

Seriously ….who invented socks? When did they appear? This awesome invention probably co-evolved in multiple world locations. Such elegant technology, that is so under-rated, dismissed and ignored for its abundant returns of comfort, pain prevention, subliminal satisfaction, continues to do the job. Students could research this simple but glorious garment, perhaps comparing what's possible with them and without them in winter, gathering social science data, experimenting with how they relate to overall body warmth, or conducting surveys about fabric, fashion, and elasticity.

Action research like this is possible with other simple objects and ideas to which children can relate.

You Could Fall Down Dizzy

Who thought up teaching six sections of the same class over and over in one day? By sixth period, I'm hard-pressed to function:

" Did I already tell this class that a Finback whale washed up on the Raritan Bay shore?"

" Is she nuts? She can't remember that?" (student thoughts/comments)

" Did I collect your homework yet?"

" Did I return your homework yet?"

" Did I tell this class about the field trip?"

Again the Prussian military model...

I am close to leaving the lab at 6 p.m. from washing beakers for 120 students. No wonder there are few science teachers. Oh, you say, "The students should be washing out the beakers. . . ." They did. They really tried. I'm just working on the "almost clean ones," drying them, putting them away, and organizing the lab.

You're Never More than Ten Feet from a Spider

"Stream studies and butterfly studies are my favorite lessons. I don't have a stream on the school grounds nor do I have a meadow. As a science teacher, I know that students need to be engaged with real things." I wrote that when I first made the great switch from a suburban to an urban school setting. I made an urban meadow in order to raise butterflies and study invertebrates, and with the help of a respected dear colleague, a courtyard garden with flowers and vegetables. These were and are showy and impressive, but not mandatory. Wherever you are, you're never more than ten feet from a spider, so we obviously studied lots of spiders. We even had yellow caution tape in the classroom, when we discovered *Araneus diadematus* traversing a large classroom window daily, some days with a brand-new web. *Tegenaria domestica,* or common house spider, is the more available and abundant near ceilings and corners of rooms. We've studied, documented, tallied, graphed, and kept baseline data for spiders and other urban wildlife: blue jays, eastern gray squirrels, monarch butterflies, cynthia moths, etc. Native and alien plant species grow everywhere from sidewalk cracks to roadside arrays and can be a wealth of information in their own right but for botany facts in general. Which were used by the pioneers and for what? What shapes and forms do they reveal? What phylum, class, order, family, and genus? My favorite urban living subjects are the lichen family with all their intricate, graceful, lacy adornments. Some students can identify *Parmelia sulcata* more and more often. I am happy when students can match three different lichens easily. Discrimination skills like this make for elated, confident moments. Powerful subjects are plentiful if a teacher can open his senses. Binge-learning is what results when your environment is taken seriously and worthy of genuine investigations.

I once rented a space for a one-room school in a church. The classroom was half underground. The window sills connected to a drainage area, then there were about thirty-six inches more to a wall. It provided the room with some light. No sooner had we moved into the room when we noticed a beautiful orange phase Wood Frog looking in our window. It was safe behind the screen and must have known its escape route. Our friend, the gracious pastor of the church, remarked that we attracted it. I laughed but disagreed that this phenomenon is just a matter of paying attention.

EMBERS

It's Possible

Our American Culture has failed at making an institution that allows **all** young humans to flourish, but we have succeeded with a few other endeavors that are wildly successful as educational models: assisted living, public libraries, beach days, summer sleep-away camps, freshman college retreats, environmental centers, museums, adult education, YouTube, paid internships, "going fishing," National Public Radio, Earthwatch, SciStarter, knitting circles, barber shops, chess clubs, and more.

Those instructive and inspirational frameworks hit the mark.

Sure . . . Ask What Culture Is Respected in My Classroom....

If you ask
What and which culture
Is respected in
My Classroom
I will tell you the culture of:
Using weather instruments,
Recipe-chemistry and moon phases,
Spiders and restroom pipes,
Magnets and
Motors turning by mini-solar panels
Telescopes and homemade sundials,
Harvesting city peas,
Decisions with topo maps,
"Catching" spectrums with
A prism and a window,
Knowing "our" river ….
Did lava make our hill?
Shush ….there's a Redtail
In the canopy
Of the Pin oak ….
"I get the leaf litter today!"
Telling the teacher to
Turn on the peregrine webcam,
Quartz is a 7?
"It's a similar trilobite!"
"The migration is happening!"
"How did I make that circuit board so warm?"
"Can we …..?"
Love that Australopithecus guy...
Breathe it, Be it
Wood sorrel is not clover

Wash it first, then eat those
Lemony heart-shaped leaves
Finding stars in constellations on night hikes and
Finding every star in the science culture.

WRAP UP: *Thoughts, audacious proclamations, and courteous edicts.*

1. Kids must engage in authentic learning. Good teachers can create it out of NOTHING, because it's everywhere:

   a. Walk around the block in January. Make a diagram of where all the nests are located. Decide whether they are made of sticks, moss, mud, etc. Analyze which species made it. Identify all or some of the trees too.

   b. Make certain that every kid knows everything about the nearest historic building, inside and out. (Age eight and up)

   c. Almost every reductionist subject can be extracted from "Current Events." (Age eight and up)

2. Earth literacy is a very high priority. Although kids don't need to know that it might be too late for humans; foster it for the pill bugs.

3. Symbolism

   a. When more emphasis is put on the little straight lines and curved lines of encoding information than the information itself, education is fraudulent.

   b. Reading programs should begin at age seven, and mostly use of Horizontal Curriculum before that.

4. Authorship is a profound act. You must have full investment in the subject to want to share it with the world. Enough with the "writing workshop."

5. Poverty

    a.   Poverty affects kids' health in general, and their brain health. Some kids overcome it; some don't.

    b.   Overindulged kids suffer from poverty of freedom.

6. Quiet *communion* among people you are with during the day enables happiness and learning. Break bread together and share.

7. Fostering development of actual skills that are self-pleasing is wholistically efficacious.

8. There are two kinds of people in the world: the self-motivated and the people who glide or settle in the current. Achieving a state of self-motivation is the apex of education.

9. School should follow the summer camp model, not the Prussian military model.

10. The infiltration of Native Americans and African Americans is a pointless, criminal, brutal, obscene riddle of history. Even the Vikings were one of the only ones that realized it and held back. (This type of hell, of course, goes beyond North America.)

11. Comfort and cradle the bullies as much as the bullied.

12. Children will benefit if they have the same teacher for more than one year.

13. Systems-learning trumps isolated facts. "*Your* place" is the optimal system in which to learn.

14. The great outdoors is a natural, harmless, earthy drug.

15. Learn the difference between the Horizontal and Vertical Curriculum.

16. Retaining information requires repetition.

17. The emergent curriculum is pure and transcendental. You're never more than ten feet from a spider.

18. Children's educational materials should be crafted by local people, not slick, parasitical corporations.

19. Giving children some choices promotes intellectual capacity.

20. Integrated schools are healthful schools.

21. All dialects must be respected.

22. A master teacher should be the boss of her curriculum.

23. Teachers need reasonable job descriptions.

24. Human Early Childhood has a super-soaked, thick, ultra-magical, intellectual energy that no other age group has (and should not have much interference.)

25. Teachers, especially early childhood teachers, need a living wage.

26. Good teachers have become more and more endangered. Teachers are endangered.

27. Be a world citizen.

28. Be on the planet; be in the universe. Don't exist in alloys and compounds.

29. Play, Play, Play ….and I don't mean with screens.

CITATIONS

-Adams State College (currently University). Alamosa, CO.

-American Museum of Natural History, 200 Central Park West, NYC.

-Association of NJ Environmental Educators (ANJEE) Conferences, advocacy, Hardscrabble Road, Bernardsville, NJ.

-*Avatar*. 2009. Film created and directed by James Cameron. 20th Century Studios (Walt Disney Company)

-Bernie. Bernie Sanders. b.1941, Brooklyn, NY. Vermont senator since 2007. Presidential candidate 2016 and 2020.

-Campbell, Joseph. (1904–1987) Wrote extensively on the importance of mythology, deities, and dreaming for understanding human behavior.

-City and Country School, (since 1914) 146 W. 13th Street, NYC.

-Class DOJO. Education tech company that enables many types of sharing between teachers and families.

-Cobb, Edith. 1977. *The Ecology of Imagination in Childhood. New York*: Columbia University Press.

-Coffin, William Sloane (1924-2006) **Benediction** (unsure of poem's credit)

-Czikzentmihaly, Mihaly. 2008. *Flow: The Psychology of Optimal Experience.* New York: Harper Perenniel.

-Danielson, Charlotte. These are evolving documents/forms. Framework for Teaching. Chicago. danielsongroup.org.

-Dewey, John. 1923. *How We Think.* San Francisco: BiblioBazaar (2009).

-Dunbar-Ortiz, Roxanne. 2015. *An Indigenous Peoples' History of the United States (REVISIONING HISTORY)*. Boston: Beacon Press.

-Duyff, Roberta Larson. 2006. *American Dietetic Association Complete Food and Nutrition Guide*. New York: Wiley.

-Earthwatch. An international organization that matches PhD researchers with students and citizen volunteers, in person, on location. Earthwatch.org. Boston, Mass.

-Emdin, Christopher. 2016. *For White Folks Who Teach in the Hood... and the rest of Y'all too: Reality Pedagogy and Urban Education*. Boston: Beacon Press.

-Essex County Environmental Center. Nature center, classes, camps, trails. Eagle Rock Ave., Roseland, NJ.

-Friends of Great Swamp. Nature center, store, trails, advocacy. New Vernon, NJ.

-Gardner, Howard. 2006. *Multiple Intelligences: New Horizons in Theory and Practice*. New York: Basic Books.

-Gatto, John Taylor. 1992. *Dumbing Us Down: The Hidden Curriculum of Compulsory Schooling*. Gabriola Island, British Columbia: New Society Publishers.

-Genesis Farm, authentic, spiritual, organic farm and learning center. Blairstown, NJ.

-Geraldine R. Dodge Foundation. Morristown, NJ.

-Glencoe. Major textbook publishing company. (one of three)

-Goodnough, Abby. 2018. "In Rehab, Two Warring Factions; Abstinence vs. Medication." (Debating the Use of Drugs to Curb the Use of Drugs) *NYTimes* 12/29/18.

-Google classroom. Platform that enables and supports assignment creation as well as sharing and grading.

-Great Swamp Outdoor Education Center. Classes, trails, nature center. Southern Boulevard, Chatham, NJ.

-Great Swamp Watershed Association. Classes, advocacy Morristown, NJ.

-Green, Maxine.(1917-2014) Teacher's College professor and theorist who promoted the arts as a fundamental learning tool. The Maxine Green Institute promotes aesthetic education and social imagination.

-Hackensack Meadowlands. Former landfill converted and landscaped into a natural setting with nature trails and kayaking and a view of the NYC skyline.

-Hakim, Joy. Author of sequential history books for children using narrative stories.

-Heine, Heinrich (1797-1856) (Visionary, German poet and philosopher)

-Hendrick, Joanne. 1988. *The Whole Child: Developmental Education for the Early Years.* New York: Pearson.

-Hill, Dorothy M. 1977. *Mud, Sand, and Water*. Washington D.C.: National Association for the Education of Young Children.

-Horwitz, Tony. 2008. *A Voyage Long and Strange: Rediscovering the New World.* New York: Henry Holt.

-James, Aaron. 2018. *Surfing with Sartre: An Aquatic Inquiry into a Life of Meaning.* New York: Anchor.

-Kohn, Alfie. 1999. *Punished by Rewards: The Trouble With Gold Stars, Incentive Plans, A's, Praise and Other Bribes.* Boston: Houghton Mifflin.

-Levitt, Steven and Stephen Dubner. 2015. *Freakonomics: A Rogue Economist Explores the Hidden Side of Everything.* Boston: Beacon Press.

-Linnaean classification: kingdom, phylum, class, order, family, genus, species. Originally developed by Carolus Linnaeus.

-Lord Stirling Environmental Education Center. Classes, nature center, trails, library, store. Whitebridge Road, Basking Ridge, NJ.

-Miller, Ron. 2006. "Reflecting on Spirituality in Education." *Encounter.*

-Monarch Teacher Network. A group of teachers who volunteer to be advocates for monarchs and all of nature. monarchteachernetwork.org

-NJ Audubon. Field trips, camps, trails, advocacy, store. Hardscrabble Rd., Bernardsville, NJ.

-NJ DEP's Sedge Island. Teacher training center. Pedagogy, marine science. Lacy Township, NJ.

-Olmstead, Frederick Law. 1822–1903. Together with Calvert Vaux, designed urban parks.

-Piaget, Jean. 1996. *A Piaget Primer: How a Child Thinks:* Revised edition. New York: Penguin Plume.

-PBwiki. A commercial collaborative editing system, currently called Pbworks. Created by David Weekly in 2005. Privately hosted wikis are for sharing files and managing projects.

-Progressive Science Initiative (PSI) from the NJ Center for Teaching and Learning. Free digital sequential content aligned to state standards for use with interactive whiteboards with digital or printed materials for students. Emphasis on group interaction. njctl.org.

-Ravitch, Diane. 2014. *Reign of Error: The Hoax of the Privatization Movement and the Danger to America's Public Schools.* New York: Vintage.

-Ridley, Matt. 2016. *The Evolution of Everything: How New Ideas Emerge.* New York: Harper.

-Schierloh, Jerry. Developed ECOLOGICAL ADDRESS, for School of Conservation, Branchville, NJ.

-School Improvement Grant. The Obama Administration offered federal funds to failing schools with strict rules or government consultant-approved methods on how the money could be spent.

-School of Conservation. Camp, classes, teacher and general learning center. Branchville, NJ

-SciStarter. An organization that matches scientists and citizens who then collect data for the scientists from the citizen's own location.

-Seeds of Peace. Summer camp in Maine for Israeli and Palestinian teens since 1993. United States Institute of Peace. usip.org

-Smartboard. Interactive white boards. Smart Technologies. Calgary.

-Sobel, David. 2004. *Place Based Education: Connecting Classrooms and Communities.* Great Barrington, Mass. Orion Society.

-Sprout House. Currently a Nursery, childcare, kindergarten, and summer day camp. From 1986–2000 an elementary school. Chatham, NJ.

-Student Growth Objectives (SGO). Specific, measurable, academic goals for students set by their teachers in consultation with their supervisors. Used emphatically as a tool to evaluate teacher performance. NJ Department of Education.

-Swimme, Brian. 2019. *The Hidden Heart of the Cosmos.* Maryknoll, NY: Orbis.

-TKCalifornia. (Transitional Kindergarten). Tkcalifornia.org.

-Waterloo Village, Stanhope, NJ. NJ State Park with a restored nineteenth century village and a replica of a thirteenth century Lenape settlement on an island in the Muskonetcong River.

-Wetlands Institute, marine nature center, classes, trails, store. Stone Harbor, NJ

-Wilshire, Bruce. 1998. *Wild Hunger: The Primal Roots of Modern Addiction.* Lanham, Md.: Rowman & Littlefield.

-White Savior Complex. Critical description of a white person who is depicted as liberating, uplifting, and rescuing non-white people. It is considered offensive because whites have been engaged and active in colonization and oppression of non-whites and should take no credit for rectification.

-Wired Magazine. Focuses on technology's effects on politics, culture and the economy. Owned by Conde Nast since 1993. San Francisco.

-Worthen, Molly. 2017. "How Memorizing Poems Pays Dividends." *NYTimes.* 9/4/17.